Contents

Native American Political Systems and the Evolution of Democracy

An Annotated Bibliography

Compiled by
Bruce E. Johansen

Bibliographies and Indexes in American History, Number 32

Greenwood Press
Westport, Connecticut • London

Library of Congress Cataloging-in-Publication Data

Johansen, Bruce E. (Bruce Elliott).
  Native American political systems and the evolution of democracy :
an annotated bibliography / compiled by Bruce E. Johansen.
      p.   cm.—(Bibliographies and indexes in American history,
  ISSN 0742–6828 ; no. 32)
  Includes index.
  ISBN 0–313–30010–0 (alk. paper)
  1. Iroquois Indians—Politics and government—Bibliography.
  2. Indians of North America—Politics and government—Bibliography.
  3. United States—Civilization—Indian influences—Bibliography.
  4. United States—Politics and government—To 1775—Bibliography.
  5. United States—Historiography—Bibliography.   I. Title.
  II. Series.
  Z1210.I7J65   1996
  [E99.I7]
  016.973'04975—dc20   96–5541

British Library Cataloguing in Publication Data is available.

Library of Congress Catalog Card Number: 96–5541
ISBN: 0–313–30010–0
ISSN: 0742–6828

First published in 1996

Greenwood Press, 88 Post Road West, Westport, CT 06881
An imprint of Greenwood Publishing Group, Inc.

Printed in the United States of America

The paper used in this book complies with the
Permanent Paper Standard issued by the National
Information Standards Organization (Z39.48–1984).

10 9 8 7 6 5 4 3 2 1

Preface

Since 1992, I have kept a bibliography of commentary on assertions that the Haudenosaunee (Iroquois) and other Native American confederacies helped shape ideas of democracy in the early United States. By 1995, the bibliography had reached roughly 455 items from more than 120 books, as well as newspaper articles and book reviews numbering in the hundreds, academic journals, films, speeches, documentaries, and other sources. The bibliography was assembled with the help of friends, as well as searches of libraries and book stores, and personal involvement in various skirmishes of the debate. The number of references exploded during 1995 because I began to search several electronic databases.

Before I explored these databases, I had been acquainted with the spread of the idea on a more personal level, especially through debates in academia that have been chronicled with Donald A. Grinde, Jr. in *Akwe:kon Journal* (now *Native Americas*) and the *American Indian Culture & Research Journal* (1993.014, 1990.002). Now, I was watching the idea take on an animus of its own, detached from its scholarly moorings. As the debate expanded in popular consciousness, a grand cacophony of diverse voices debated the type of history with which we will enter a new millennium on the Christian calendar.

I watched as the idea became part of the written record in several academic fields, as well as in many journals of popular discourse. Everyone -- from Tom Hayden (1994.012) to Patrick Buchanan (1992.037, 1992.056) and Rush Limbaugh (1992.019) -- seemed to have taken a stand on what had become a very hotly contested issue. These ideas became a horror story of political correctness to many conservative commentators, while they also played a role in Canadian debates over a new constitution. I found Iroquois ideas of democracy being applied to contemporary problems by a wide range of thinking people, from historians, to lawyers and judges, to political scientists, artists, musicians, and engineers.

I compiled my bibliography with a sense of awe, having taken up the idea as a newspaper reporter in Seattle twenty years ago at the behest of a Native American student, Sally Fixico, at the Evergreen State College in Olympia. With research help from Phil Lucas, a Choctaw film maker, I undertook a Ph.D. dissertation detailing how Benjamin Franklin and Thomas Jefferson had perceived Native American societies, particularly at the political system of the Iroquois, who call themselves Haudenosaunee, or "The People of the Longhouse." The dissertation became *Forgotten Founders* (1975.013, 1987.004). As I wrote the dissertation, I found similar work (1975.010) by Donald A. Grinde, Jr., a Yamasee and historian. We met during several mutual speaking engagements in the late 1980s, and co-authored *Exemplar of Liberty* (1991.004).

The ideas in our books engendered a fair amount of controversy in academia, and in the popular press. By 1992, I took a long look at a growing stack of documentary evidence in my office, and decided that the time had come to compile a bibliography. As a student of communication (my primary teaching field), I was fascinated by the spread of the idea, and how so many different people could take so many varying points of view all at once. While the books that Grinde and I have published on this subject trace the ways in which American Indian confederacies helped to shape democratic thought into the nineteenth century, this bibliography is meant to trace the debate over this issue into our own time. A raucous debate grew up around the idea after 1987, as Cornell University's American Indian Program held its watershed conference on the issue. Debate over the issue also was boosted that year by commemorations of the U.S. Constitution's bicentennial. In 1992, the debate was heightened by remembrances of Columbus' first voyages. At the same time, the issue of Iroquois influence on democracy was becoming an issue of argument in debates over multiculturalism and "political correctness."

Even as the debate exploded after 1987, I found a number of older references. President John F. Kennedy advocated Iroquois influence on Benjamin Franklin in a book published during 1961 (Brandon, 1900.004, 1900.005); Charles Eastman, the Lakota Sioux author, made the case for Native American shaping of democratic thought in 1919 (1900.025). Anthropologist Clark Wissler raised the idea in 1940 (1900.021). Historian Julian Boyd (who edited Jefferson's papers) made a case for it in 1942 (1900.003). Paul A.W. Wallace, an English professor and long-time student of the Iroquois, contended in

1945 that the United Nations was based in part on an Iroquois model (1900.020). Mohawk educator and activist Tehanetorens (Ray Fadden) advanced the idea about 1950 (1900.017, 1900.025). In 1952, Felix Cohen, author of the *Handbook of Indian Law,* made an evocative case that American Indian notions of liberty fired the national imagination (1900.006). Author Alvin Josephy raised the issue in 1958 (1900.010), and literary journalist Edmund Wilson treated it briefly in his 1960 title *Apologies to the Iroquois* (1900.021).

Before the "influence" idea became widely popular, it was part of the script for "Night of the First Americans" (1975.026), a stage play which was performed March 4, 1982 at the Kennedy Center for the Performing Arts, Washington, D.C. The script was written by Phil Lucas and included performances by a number of well-known Indian and non-Indian actors and artists, such as Lorne Greene, Will Sampson, Jonathan Winters, Vincent Price, Paul Ortega, Ironeyes Cody, Martin Sheen, Dennis Weaver, Loretta Lynn, Dick Cavett, Hoyt Axton, Will Rogers, Jr., Kevin Locke, and Wayne Newton. The performance contained a substantial segment outlining the Iroquois role in the formulation of U.S. democracy.

The idea of Iroquois influence on the development of democracy has drawn a large number of conservative critics who have turned the idea into a purported horror story of multiculturalism and "political correctness." Many of these critics reduce the assertion to a shorthand (for example, by denying that the founders "copied the Constitution" from the Iroquois), with little reference to the fact that the issue has engaged a debate which has produced a considerable literature. Rather, these critics breeze in and out of the subject as if it were cocktail-party conversation.

In his *Forbes* column "Keeping Up," for example, Daniel Seligman (1993.057) took aim at "political correctness," which he described as "a movement driven by truly totalitarian impulses, [which] is embodied in thought police who endlessly endeavor to suppress data...." Seligman then hauls out the issue of Iroquois influence on the Constitution as his primary exhibit of "politically correct" thought, which he linked to a general decline in American educational levels as reflected in Scholastic Aptitude Test scores. He called assertions of influence "fatuous." Seligman quoted Arthur Schlesinger, Jr.'s *Disuniting of America* (1992.024), a short polemic turned out quickly by a liberal historian whom conservative reviewers embraced fervently. In *The Disuniting of America,* Schlesinger took issue with "history for self-esteem," or "feel-good history," by which, he said, self-interested minority groups seek to express their points of view in school curricula. This point of view was not invented by Schlesinger. Several conservative commentators had used it before him. For example, George Will (1991.038 1993.061), made Iroquois influence an example of "feel-good history" in his syndicated columns in *Newsweek* and hundreds of newspapers. At one point, he called it "fiction."

In its most extreme form, this political-correctness horror story is sometimes held responsible for just about every uncivilized evil to befall Europe since the barbarians took down the Roman Empire. Dead European White Males (DEWMs) roll in their graves at the sound of the "influence" issue, according to some English commentators (1991.017, 1992.041, 1993.042). Orlando *Sentinel* columnist Charley Reese (1994.047) wrote that ideas such as Iroquois influence on democracy lay a claim on gullible Americans because they don't know their own history. His version of history is simple: "*All* the institutions of American government are derived from our European culture. *None* comes from Africa or Asia or American Indians....The superbly educated authors of the American Revolution had nothing to learn from a primitive tribal alliance." [emphasis added] Since their perceptual framework admits to no hint of non-European influence on the evolution of democracy, Reese and others tend to believe the whole school of thought has been fabricated for political reasons. In *Forbes* magazine, Dinesh D'Souza, a research fellow at the American Enterprise Institute, targeted "a new barbarism -- dogmatic, intolerant, and oppressive" that he asserted had "descended on America's institutions of higher learning...a neo-Marxist ideology promoted in the name of multiculturalism" (1991.018). An example of such thinking, wrote D'Souza, was the idea "that the Iroquois Indians in America had a representative democracy which served as a model for the American system." D'Souza's uninformed bombast imitated earlier comments by Richard Grenier, columnist for the Washington *Times* (1990.013, 1990.014, 1991.020), and John Leo, commentator for *U.S. News & World Report* (1990.020, 1994.042).

The "influence" idea has worked into discourse in a number of academic fields, among them Native American Studies, American History, Anthropology, Law, Education, and Political Science. R. David Edmunds, in "Native Americans, New Voices: American Indian History, 1895-1995," surveys developments in American history relating to Native Americans during the century since the *American Historical Review* began publishing in 1895. Edmunds commented that "Recently, claims by some Native American historians that the Constitution of the United States was modelled after the Iroquois Confederacy have attracted the public's attention and engendered considerable controversy" (1995.007).

James A. Joseph, in *Remaking America: How the Benevolent Traditions of Many Cultures Are Transforming Our National Life,*

[1995] begins the first page of his first chapter by quoting from *Exemplar of Liberty* [1991]: "The native peoples lived in confederations so subtle, so nearly invisible, as to be an attractive alternative to monarchy's overbearing hand" (1995.014). The author then writes, "The advanced democratic practices of the Iroquois, for example, fitted very well with the abstract principles of democracy already forming in the minds of the European settlers." Joseph also cites Karl Marx on Iroquois governance, as well as Benjamin Franklin and Tom Paine. Joseph was president and chief executive officer of the Council on Foundations, an umbrella group for U.S. charitable foundations, when he wrote this book. In July, 1995, Joseph was nominated as ambassador to South Africa by President Clinton.

The "influence" thesis has been incorporated to some degree in the general study of American colonial history. An example is provided by Arthur Quinn's *New World: An Epic of Colonial America From the Founding of Jamestown to the Fall of Quebec* (1994.020). Quinn is a professor of rhetoric at the University of California. In this book, he outlines the founding legend of the Iroquois Confederacy and argues that it helped shape the United States. He presents events involving Benjamin Franklin and the Iroquois in some detail, beginning with the Iroquois leader Cannassatego's advice that the colonists unite on an Iroquois model at the Lancaster Treaty Council in 1744. Within the scholarly literature of law, Renee Jacobs (1991.006) reviewed the Iroquois Great Law of Peace in relation to "how the founding fathers ignored the clan mothers." She made a case that as the founders adapted some aspects of Iroquois law, they were nearly totally blind to the equity of the sexes that was woven into Haudenosaunee fundamental law and political life. Author Paula Gunn Allen has addressed similar themes (1988.001). Feminist historian Sally Roesch Wagner has explored the influences of Iroquois society on the philosophies of Elizabeth Cady Stanton and Matilda Joslyn Gage (1988.011, 1989.014, 1992.028, 1995.020).

The literature of the debate also contains numerous references to opposition to the "influence" idea by Temple Anthropology Professor Elisabeth Tooker (1988.010, 1990.007), as well as State University of New York anthropologist William Starna (1990.025, 1991.035). The core of the ethnohistorical establishment has been opposed to the idea, in visible opposition to traditional Haudenosaunee leaders such as Oren Lyons (1992.019, 1992.020, 1992.070, 1994.043). Tooker and other opponents of the idea, such as Francis Jennings of the Newberry Library (1993.013) and former president of the American Society for Ethnohistory James Axtell (1992.003) have been joined in pointed debate on this issue by Native American scholars such as Vine Deloria, Jr. (1992.010) and Ward Churchill (1992.008, 1994.007), as well as

History Professor Wilbur Jacobs (1993.011, 1993.012, 1994.014). Macalester College Anthropology Professor Jack Weatherford's *Indian Givers* (1988.012) advocates the "influence" idea and borrows heavily from work by Grinde, Johansen, and others. In the field of ecological activism, Jerry Mander enthusiastically endorses the idea in his *In the Absence of the Sacred* (1991.011).

One illustration of the idea's disciplinary flexibility was its use by John Lienhard, a professor of engineering at the University of Houston, who is known as the host of the eclectic National Public Radio program "The Engines of our Ingenuity." The program aired its 1,000th broadcast during 1995. Lienhard mastered a stutter to broadcast his program, which includes a wide range of subject matter. He broadcasts over 30 National Public Radio affiliates in the United States. An article in the Houston *Chronicle* listed a number of segment titles. "Another dealt with what the U.S. Constitution owes to the political system of the Iroquois nation....The transcript of [this segment] is the most requested Lienhard episode to date" (1995.021).

The "influence" thesis has been taken up in some unusual places. In the magazine *Sassy*, which is intended mainly for teenaged girls, author Mary Kaye (1992.048) tucked a reference to Native American democracy among articles with titles like "Axl Rose: Clothes Horse" and "Beauty Tips for Procrastinators." The article was headlined (on the magazine's cover) "Why Our Screwed-up Planet Needs Native Americans." The issue has played a bit part on the rap-music stage (1995.024, 1993.045). Singer Buffy Sainte-Marie, who has been engaged in efforts to educate Native American young people, has publicized a belief that American Indians practiced consensus building a long time before the idea became popular in other cultures (1992.063, 1994.047). Oneida singer Joanne Shenandoah mentioned the idea as she opened the three-day 1994 Woodstock music festival, a reprise of a similar event in 1969, with a Haudenosaunee delegation before about 250,000 people (1994.029).

Native American democratic traditions have played a role in Canada's contemporary debate over what form of federalism will serve its peoples best in the future. Iroquois who live in Canada have reminded federal authorities there that they are capable of self-government, having practiced their own system under the Great Law of Peace for several centuries before Europeans arrived. On June 12, 1992, Joe Clark, President of the Privy Council and Minister Responsible for Constitutional Affairs, told the annual meeting of the Canadian Manufacturer's Association that Native Canadians have the right and responsibility to govern themselves, pointing to the Iroquois: "Aboriginal self-government...was here when Thomas Jefferson and Benjamin Franklin looked to the Iroquois Confederacy when they were designing the American Constitution" (1992.009, 1992.071). A 1993 report by Canada's Royal Commission on Aboriginal Peoples, *Partners in Confederation: Aboriginal Peoples, Self-Government, and the Constitution* (1993.024), considered alternatives to Canada's present confederation, and Native American peoples' roles in Canadian governance. Iroquois models of government are presented. The report argues that the Canadian confederation has come to resemble the Iroquois League over time, moving gradually away from exclusive reliance on its British origins.

American Indian (especially Iroquois) democratic precedents have been used in the United States to support political decentralization as a way to dissemble the "special-interest state." Tom Hayden, a founder of Students for a Democratic Society in the 1960s and a California state senator in the 1990s, called for a decentralization on "a Jeffersonian, or Quaker, or Iroquois" model in an economy based on an eco-system balanced for generations to come (1994.012). Martin W. Lewis debunked the Iroquois' example as a model for decentralization in his *Green Delusions: An Environmentalist Critique of Radical Environmentalism* (1992.018). Lewis, an assistant professor of geography at George Washington University, argued that participatory democracy may not eliminate social repression. Instead, he believes it perpetuates "a tyranny of long-winded individuals [who are] immune to boredom." Lewis found the Iroquois to be "a particularly ill-considered exemplar. Admiring the Iroquois political system of that era for its democracy is akin to praising Nazi Germany for its enlightened forestry. The Five Nations not only engaged in a highly successful campaign of ethnocide against their competitors in the fur trade, the Hurons, but they also raised the torture of war captives (those whom they chose not to adopt, at any rate) to a high art."

Even as New York State declined to publish the Haudenosaunee curriculum for its own students, the "influence idea" was permeating school curricula across the United States by the 1990s. Literature published by the second National School Celebration stressed America's patriotic heritage for several million elementary-school children, taking a decidedly multicultural tack (1994.021). The 1992 celebration was held exactly a century after the first, for which the "Pledge of Allegiance" was written. The booklet contains an essay by Elizabeth Christensen ("Our Founding Grandfathers") observing Iroquois roots of American democracy. The booklet also lists month-by-month themes for school celebrations. The theme for October is "How did the political and social order of Native Americans influence American democracy?" The "influence" idea has been treated in *Junior Scholastic* (1988.031) and in *Scholastic Update* (1989.004).

James W. Loewen spent a year at the Smithsonian surveying the 12 leading high-school history textbooks, and concluded that none of them makes history interesting. He sets out to do that in *Lies My Teacher Told Me* (1995.015). One of the themes that Loewen described (asserting that conventional histories usually ignore it) is the influence of the Iroquois' system of government on the framers of the Constitution. Loewen devotes a chapter to portrayals of Indians in high-school texts, calling them "the most lied-about subset of our population." Over the course of this chapter, he devotes considerable space to the historical circumstances that initiated Iroquois influence of U.S. political institutions.

Native American democracy has been described in Europe as well as in North America. An article in *The Warsaw Voice* (1993.019), a journal for Americans of Polish descent, described the activities of the Polish Friendship Society, a group of Poles who study American Indian history and issues, publish books, and edit a journal.

> The quarterly includes materials about the Great Peace Law, which is a discovery for the Polish reader. The law made it possible for the confederation of five Iroquois nations to function in harmony for several centuries. The editors stress that this law was taken by white colonists as a model for the United States constitution...and a model for democracy, but later the colonists forgot for long years both the Indian original and its authors.

In a similar vein, Raul Manglapus, Philippine foreign secretary, challenged the industrial world's assumptions about European primacy in shaping democracy at a ministerial meeting of the 21-nation Council of Europe at its headquarters in Strasborg, Germany. "The democratic value that is the heart of the constitution of the Council of Europe is indigenous not only to the northern societies, but to all human cultures...." According to an unsigned newspaper account from Interpress Service (1988.014), Manglapus "cit[ed] democratic republics like Licchavis, developed on the Indian subcontinent 600 years before Christ, [and] the Iroquois Confederacy that preceded the United States Constitution...." Manglapus' analysis sounds much like that of John Adams, who surveyed federal structures around the world in his *Defence of the Constitutions...* (1787), a reference used at the Constitutional Convention.

Despite its caricature as a horror story of "political correctness" and the jarring nature of some of the debate over the issue, the idea that Native American confederacies are an important early form of democracy has become established in general discourse. History is made in many ways, by many people; the spread of the idea that Native American confederacies (especially the Haudenosaunee Confederacy) helped shape the intellectual development of democracy in the United States and Europe is an example of how our notions of history have been changing with the infusion of multicultural voices. It is fascinating to watch the change in all its forms -- and the debate over the issue in all its cacophonous variety. This bibliography comprises the "field notes" of my journey.

Acknowledgments

I would like to extend my thanks to John Kahionhes Fadden, Donald A. Grinde, Jr., Jose Barreiro, Shelly Price-Jones, Sally Roesch-Wagner, Steve Witala, Scott Calbeck, Barbara Mann, and Bruce A. Burton for providing titles from their files. Many thanks also are due the incredible bibliographic sleuths of the University of Nebraska at Omaha Interlibrary Loan Office. Cynthia Harris and Jane C. Lerner of Greenwood Press also contributed to this bibliography with their sharp eyes and sage advice.

Native American Political Systems and the Evolution of Democracy

Bibliographic Entries

1995

Books, Scholarly and Specialty Journals

1995.001. Alfred, Gerald R. *Heeding the Voices of Our Ancestors: Kahnawake Mohawk Politics and the Rise of Native Nationalism.* Toronto: Oxford University Press, 1995.

This political history of the Kahnawake Mohawk reserve near Montreal contains an extensive review of traditional Iroquois political practices in chapter four. On page 78, Alfred calls the Iroquois Confederacy "the first genuine North American federal system." In two footnotes (on pages 196 and 197), Alfred directs readers to *Exemplar of Liberty* [1991] and *Forgotten Founders* [1982, 1987] for "a discussion of the [Iroquois] Confederacy in relation to its representation of democracy, and its influence on later attempts at the design of federal systems." Alfred's book is the first academic study of the modern political history of Kahnawake.

1995.002. Birchfield, Dan and Mark Sachner, eds. *The Encyclopedia of American Indians.* New York: Marshall Cavendish, in press.

This 10-volume work contains references to the influence thesis in several entries, among them "Cannassatego," "Hendrick," "Iroquois Confederacy," "Franklin, Benjamin," "Albany Plan of Union," "Deganawidah," "Native Governments," "American Revolution," "United States Constitution," *et al.* The entries were written by Bruce

Johansen. *The Encyclopedia of Native Americans* is aimed at an audience of young people

1995.003. Bruchac, Joseph, ed. *New Voices From the Longhouse.* Greenfield, N.Y.: Greenfield Press, 1995.

This collection of poetry, prose stories, and history from contemporary Haudenosaunee (Iroquois) includes a reference (on p. 217) to the examination of the Iroquois role in the development of democracy in Barreiro, ed., *Indian Roots of American Democracy* [1988, 1992].

1995.004. Calloway, Colin G. *The American Revolution in Indian Country: Crisis and Diversity in Native American Communities.* Cambridge, England: Cambridge University Press, 1995.

This book, which asserts that it is "the first broad coverage of Indian experiences in the American Revolution," briefly raises the "influence" issue on page 298: "In the propaganda of the Revolution, Indian figures and accoutrements frequently symbolized the American cause. One school of thought even maintains that Indian influence was so pervasive among the founding fathers' generation that the League of the Iroquois provided a model for the framing of the United States Constitution....Indian influences endured in the new republic, but the United States had no place for Indian people." Calloway cites Grinde and Johansen, *Exemplar of Liberty* [1991], and the Johansen-Tooker exchange in *Ethnohistory* [1990].

1995.005. Coburn, Joseph, *et al.* "American Indians," in Carl A. Grant, ed., *Educating for Diversity.* Boston: Allyn and Bacon, 1995.

Coburn, *et al.* contribute a 30-page essay on American Indians to this "anthology of multicultural voices." In the essay (on p. 239), the authors write: "The U.S. government was heavily influenced by the League of the Iroqois [*sic*]. Democracy and communist governments were influenced by the 'Village Council' governing practices utilized by the majority of tribes in pre-Columbian America. Forms of this practice survive today."

1995.006. D'Souza, Dinesh. *The End of Racism.* New York: Free Press, 1995.

Part of D'Souza's case that racism has ended rests of what he regards as liberals' "bogus multiculturalism." In this context, he agrees that Native Americans provided general society with potatoes, tomatoes, kayaks, corn, and canoes. He even approves of assertions that the phrase "OK" comes from a Native American language (probably Choctaw). However, D'Souza finds "virtually non-existent" (p. 356) support for the idea that the Iroquois political system helped shape American concepts of democracy. D'Souza cites approvingly work by Temple Anthropology Professor Elisabeth Tooker [1988], but calls her an historian and misspells her first name (as "Elizabeth"). D'Souza references one source in support of the "influence" idea: "Thomas Riley, 'History and Foodstuffs,' *National Review*, November 19, 1990." A biographical check indicated that Riley is a professor of anthropology at the University of Illinois. The purported article does not exist, at least not in *National Review*, one more indication of D'Souza's incredibly sloppy scholarship.

1995.007. Edmunds, R. David. "Native Americans, New Voices: American Indian History, 1895-1995." *American Historical Review* 100:3 (June, 1995), pp. 717-740.

This survey of developments in American history relating to Native Americans during the century since *AHR* began publishing comments, on page 729, that "Recently, claims by some Native American historians that the Constitution of the United States was modelled after the Iroquois Confederacy have attracted the public's attention and engendered considerable controversy." Edmunds references *Exemplar of Liberty* [1991], and *Exiled in the Land of the Free* [1992]. In a footnote, Edmunds writes that "...Grinde and...Johansen argued that the political theories of the 'founding fathers' were heavily influenced by their familiarity with the political structure of the Iroquois Confederacy. Their assertions have created considerable debate, and have attracted both the media, the public, and the Congress [*sic*]."

1995.008. Grinde, Donald A. and Bruce E. Johansen. *Ecocide of Native America: Environmental Destruction of Native Lands and People.* Santa Fe: Clear Light, 1995.

On page 248, Lummi Jewell Praying Wolf James notes "with irony" that American Indian confederacies and societies influenced the development of democracy in the United States. The irony, says James, is that the same nation justified the "constant taking of Indian rights, natural resources, and lands."

1995.009. Grinde, Donald A., Jr., Bruce E. Johansen, Philip A. Levy, and Samuel Payne. "Forum on Iroquois Influence on the Formation of the American Polity." *William & Mary Quarterly*, in press.

This forum was scheduled to appear in the July, 1996, issue of *WMQ*, with Grinde and Johansen arguing in support of "influence," and Levy and Payne arguing against. Levy and Payne thank James Axtell for assisting them in their efforts.

1995.010. Hauptman, Laurence. *Tribes and Tribulations: Misconceptions About American Indians and Their Histories*. Albuquerque: University of New Mexico Press, 1995.

This book contains a chapter (the third) titled "Speculations on the Constitution," in which Hauptman rues the fact that the "Trolls" have been unable to crush the pervasive "misconception" that the Iroquois and other Native American confederations helped shape democracy. "Despite the highly speculative nature of the evidence" [Hauptman reviews very little of it], "this misconception has become a shibboleth," writes the author, citing the U.S. Senate resolution of 1988 supporting the idea. Hauptman speculates that the Iroquois created oral history to assert that key ideas were borrowed from them. He concentrates mainly on James Wilson, arguing that he was too materialistic and Euro-centric to appreciate the Iroquois example. As he makes his case, Hauptman ignores this quote from Wilson at the Constitutional convention: "The British government cannot be our model. We have no materials for a similar one. Our manners, our laws, the abolition of entails and primogeniture, the whole genius of the people are opposed to it." This book cites Grinde and Johansen, *Exemplar of Liberty* [1991], Grinde [1977], Johansen [1982, 1987], *Exiled in the Land of the Free* [1992], and other proponents of "influence."

1995.011. Hirschfelder, Arlene, ed. *Native Heritage: Personal Accounts by American Indians, Past and Present.* New York: MacMillan, 1995.

On pp. 165-166, Sarah Winnemucca, a Pauite, describes her peoples' decision-making processes, and says, "We have a republic as well as you. The council-tent is our Congress, and any anybody can speak who has anything to say, women and all....If women could go into Congress, I think justice would be done to the Indians." This was originally published in Sarah Winnemucca Hopkins, *Life Among the Paiutes: Their Wrongs and Claims.* New York: G.P. Putnam's Sons, 1883.

1995.012. Howard, Jean, with Margaret Rubin. *Manual for the Peacemaker.* Wheaton, Illinois: Quest Books, 1995

This book traces the story of Deganawidah and Hiawatha. and includes exercises designed to make the Peacemaker's teachings useful to all. In its introduction (on pp. xxii and xxiii), Howard discusses ways in which Iroquois political thought helped shape that of Franklin, Jefferson, in the United States, as well as French and British philosophers. Howard quotes from Johansen, *Forgotten Founders* [1982, 1987] and Felix Cohen, "Americanizing the White Man" [1952].

1995.013. Johansen, Bruce E. and Donald A. Grinde, Jr. *The Encyclopedia of Native American Biography.* New York: Henry Holt, in press.

This compilation of about 700 Native American biographies includes references to the influence idea under "Cannassatego," Hendrick," "Franklin, Benjamin," and others.

1995.014. Joseph, James A. *Remaking America: How the Benevolent Traditions of Many Cultures Are Transforming Our National Life.* San Francisco: Jossey-Bass Publishers, 1995.

Joseph writes, on p. 23: "The advanced democratic practices of the Iroquois, for example, fitted very well with the abstract principles of democracy already forming in the minds of the European settlers." On pp. 25-26, Joseph cites Karl Marx on Iroquois governance, as well as Benjamin Franklin and Tom Paine. In addition to *Exemplar*, he cites

Weatherford, *Indian Givers* [1988]. Joseph, president and chief executive officer of the Council on Foundations, in 1995 was nominated as ambassador to South Africa by President Clinton.

1995.015. Loewen, James W. *Lies My Teacher Told Me.* New York: The New Press, 1995.

Loewen spent a year at the Smithsonian surveying the 12 leading high-school history textbooks, and concluded that none of them make history interesting. He sets out to do that in *Lies My Teacher Told Me*. One of the themes that he describes (asserting that conventional histories usually ignore it) is "the influence of the Iroquois' system of government on the framers of the Constitution." [review, San Francisco *Chronicle*, below]. Loewen devotes Chapter 4 to portrayals of Indians in high-school texts, calling them "the most lied-about subset of our population." (p. 92) Over the course of this chapter, he devotes considerable space to the historical circumstances that initiated Iroquois influence of U.S. political institutions; in a footnote (p. 328), Loewen takes issue with Arthur Schlesinger, Jr.'s argument in *Disuniting of America* [1992] that Europe was "also the source -- the *unique* source -- of those liberating ideas of individual liberty." Comments Loewen: "He offers no evidence, only assertion, for this claim, and apparently does not know of Europe's astonishment not only at Native American liberty but also at religious freedom in China And Turkey." Loewen says that when Spain expelled the Moors in 1492, Turkey offered them sanctuary.

1995.016. Mac Donald, Heather. "The Sobol Report: Multiculturalism Triumphant." In Hilton Kramer and Roger Kimball, *Against the Grain: The New Criterion on Art and Intellect at the End of the Twentieth Century.* Chicago: Ivan R. Dee, 1995.

In this collection of essays from the neo-conservative journal *The New Criterion*, Mac Donald decries the Sobol Report ("The Curriculum of Inclusion") in New York State as a product of racial (mainly black) politics, resulting in the destruction of historical standards. She simplifies the thrust of multiculturalism to a banal slogan: "Hey hey, ho, ho, western culture's gotta go!" Along the way, she argues, by the time the multiculturalists have replaced European books with video tapes of African artifacts in schools, "if the multiculturalists amass enough power, they could find not just Iroquois but Egyptian influence on the Constitution." This piece of *reductio ad absurdum* denial is an aside in a longer polemic against Martin Bernal's *Black Athena* and other arguments that African thinking influenced Europe.

1995.017. *Magill Ready Reference: American Indians.* Anaheim, CA: Salem Press, 1995.

The Iroquois political system is examined in a lengthy entry on "Political Organization and Leadership," by Johansen.

1995.018. Mintz, Steven. "A Guide to Recent Books in Native American History." *American Indian Quarterly* 19:1 (Winter, 1995), pp. 91-142.

Forgotten Founders [1982, 1987], *Exemplar of Liberty* [1991] and *Exiled in the Land of the Free* [1992] are among the books listed in this bibliography of Native American history. The use of "recent" here is relative; some of the cited titles were published as early as 1948.

1995.019. Volokh, Alexander. "The Green Crusade: Rethinking the Roots of Environmentalism." [book review] *Reason*, 26:10 (March, 1995), p. 62.

Volokh belittles Peter Marshall's *Nature's Web: Rethinking Our Place on Earth* [1994], which posits the Native American belief that human beings are part of a web of life in which all things share spiritual connection. He smirks as he lists Marshall's "favorite philosophers...the Taoists, the Iroquois, and Immanuel Kant." Volokh argues, *reductio ad absurdum*, that at least Marshall stops short of advocating "stones' rights."

1995.020. Wagner, Sally Roesch. "The Untold Iroquois Influence on Early Feminists." *On the Issue*, November, 1995 [in press].

How did nineteenth-century feminists Matilda Joslyn Gage and Elizabeth Cady Stanton arrive at their vision of a world in which relations between the sexes would be transformed? They didn't get it from the patriarchal society in which they lived, Wagner argues. Instead, both feminists lived in Upstate New York and studied the matrilineal society of the Iroquois Confederacy. Wagner traces the ways in which the lives of Iroquois women affected the world views of these three important feminists.

Newspaper and Magazine Articles

1995.021. Ackerman, Todd. "Being Creative About Others' Creativity; University of Houston Professor John Lienhard celebrates the Human Side of Technology..." Houston *Chronicle*, March 12, 1995, p. A-33.

Lienhard is known as the host of an eclectic National Public Radio program "The Engines of our Ingenuity," which recently celebrated its 1,000th broadcast. Lienhard, a professor of engineering, mastered a stutter to broadcast his program. He broadcasts over 30 NPR affiliates nationwide. The article lists a number of segment titles. "...Another dealt with what the U.S. Constitution owes to the political system of the Iroquois nation....The transcript of [this segment] is the most requested Lienhard episode to date."

1995.022. Barreiro, Jose. "Bigotshtick: Rush Limbaugh on Indians." *Native Americas*, Fall, 1995, pp. 40-43.

Barreiro, editor-in-chief of *Native Americas*, concludes an analysis of Rush Limbaugh's anti-Indian rhetoric: "It may be wise to keep watch on the bigoted views of Rush Limbaugh. Because he serves as a barometer of the national climate, familiarity with the points of attack can be useful. But remember also this truth: Native Americans...carried out a prescribed protocol of participatory democracy....This style of governance spawned confederacies and produced a palpable freedom...that inspired colonial leaders, and *that* is more 'of America' than Rush Limbaugh...."

1995.023. Bradley, Bill. "Democracy's 'Third Leg.'" *Christian Science Monitor*, February 27, 1995.

In an opinion column, the former basketball star and current Democratic U.S. senator from New Jersey, calls for increased citizen activism. He deplores the fact that money plays such a large role in access to today's political arena. "From the Longhouse of the Iroquois to the general store of de Tocqueville's America, to the Chautauquas...Americans have always had places where they could come together and deliberate their common future."

1995.024. Britton, Bonnie. "'Indian' Out of the 'Cupboard,' Into Motivation." Indianapolis *Star*, July 21, 1995, p. E-1.

Litefoot, a 26-year-old member of the Cherokee Nation, plays Little Bear, an Onondaga who is taken from 1761 to the present in the movie "The Indian in the Cupboard." Litefoot, who calls himself the "first Native American rap artist/motivator," is described in this interview as "fiercely devoted to promoting cultural identity and awareness among young Native Americans." Britton writes that "...He's no fan of Custer (a punk) or George Washington (an Indian killer) or Benjamin Franklin, who he says plagiarized from the Iroquois Confederacy 'and put it in the Constitution.'" The "influence" issue also is mentioned briefly in the script of the movie.

1995.025. D'Souza, Dinesh. "Multicultural Lies My Teacher Taught Me." Arizona *Republic* [Phoenix], Perspective, September 24, 1995, p. F-1.

D'Souza, author of *The End of Racism* [1995], writes that assertions of Iroquois "as founding fathers" is an exercise in "misrepresentation, bordering on falsehood" and "bogus multiculturalism." He makes the same case with reference to assertions that the "three-fifths" clause in the Constitution was a dehumanization of black slaves. On "influence," D'Souza cites Alvin Josephy, Jr. and Jack Weatherford in support, and "historian Elizabeth Tooker" (he means *anthropologist* Elisabeth Tooker) in opposition. He argues that Tooker limits the case to one quote (Franklin's 1751 letter to his printing partner James Parker), which she does not, as he tries to simplify the issue to absurdity, a common tactic of conservative critics.

1995.026. George, Doug (Kanentiio). "Iroquois Have Good Reason to See Positives in Fourth of July." Syracuse *Herald-American*, July 2, 1995.

"We Iroquois have mixed feelings regarding this day," George says of the Fourth of July. "We are concerned that the lessons in democracy our ancestors taught the Founding Fathers have not yet been fully realized." George notes the impact of the Iroquois at the Albany Congress of 1754, and writes: "It is now well established that Franklin, Thomas Jefferson, John Hancock, George Washington, John Adams, and James Monroe studied the Iroquois manner of government in order to mine its concepts for their own use." Iroquois feelings about the Fourth are mixed because George Washington's armies devastated lands of those who sided with the British in the American Revolution.

1995.027. Huntington, Richard. "A View of the World from an Iroquois Perspective." Buffalo *News*, January 11, 1995, Lifestyles, p. 7.

Huntington, the *News'* art critic, reviews a show by 24 Iroquois artists at Niagara University. He begins the review by noting that the United States adopted the eagle which soars overhead the Iroquois Great Tree of Peace "as its symbol for freedom and democracy."

1995.028. Johansen, Bruce E. "Dating the Iroquois Confederacy." *Akwesasne Notes*, New Series 1:3 & 4 (Fall, 1995) pp. 62-63.

This article describes work done by Barbara Mann, a Ph.D. student at Toledo University, and Jerry Fields, an astronomer, which indicates that the Iroquois Confederacy was founded in 1142 A. D., three centuries before the contemporary scholarly consensus. The date is based on the occurrence of a total solar eclipse after which the Senecas adopted the Great Peace. The article notes that the Iroquois Confederacy has been called a forerunner of United States institutions.

1995.029. Karash, Julius A. "Program Helps Indian Youths." Kansas City *Star*, August 20, 1995, p. A-1.

This front-page story begins by contrasting the number of Indian-derived names around Kansas City (such as "Arrowhead Stadium, home of the Chiefs") with the poverty and neglect of 7,000 Native Americans who live in the urban area. It describes the work of Visible Horizons, which "works to help Indian youths claim their piece of the American Dream and reclaim pride in their heritage." The article describes a class taught by Carol Lee Sanchez-Allen at the Bader Memorial Christian Church, which outlines Native American contributions to American culture, including "the Iroquois Confederacy's concept of Grand Council [which] influenced Benjamin Franklin's ideas for the U.S. Constitution."

1995.030. Mackey, Mary. "Everything Your American History Textbook Got Wrong" [review of James Loewen, *Lies My Teacher Told Me*]. San Francisco *Chronicle*, February 12, 1995, p. 3.

1995.031. May, Pamela. [Review of Awiakta, *Selu: Seeking the Corn Mother's Wisdom*] *Whole Earth Review*, June 22, 1995, p. 74.

May describes Awaikta's book as "a potent offering of Native American wisdom." This review includes a brief account of the Iroquois Great Law of Peace, observing that it was used as "a primary model for the [U. S.] Constitution." May writes that "Benjamin Franklin and his colleagues" studied the Great Law.

1995.032. "Mohawks Look at Constitution." Associated Press in Plattsburgh [N. Y.] *Press-Republican*, April 8, 1995.

Discussing a new written constitution for Akwesasne Mohawks under United States jurisdiction, P. J. Herne, acting coordinator of the St. Regis Mohawk Tribal Courts Program, is quoted as saying: "There's a long-standing debate in academia [as to] whether the U.S. Constitution is based on Iroquois democracy." Ironically, the "elective" system was created two centuries ago by New York State to replace the original Mohawk council, which still operates at Akwesasne. Akwesasne Mohawk John Kahionhes Fadden, who supplied this piece, commented: "These 'elective' Mohawks appear blinded to the fact that they already have a constitution -- *Kaianerekowa* [The Great Law of Peace]."

1995.033. Nolan, Maureen. "Iroquois Women Serve as Models." Syracuse *Post-Standard*, April 8, 1995, p. B-3.

This article surveys the matrilineal nature of traditional Iroquois society, and asserts that nineteenth century feminists such as Stanton and Gage used Iroquois examples in their critique of patriarchy. "Contemporary feminist scholar Sally Roesch Wagner argues that...'They studied the Iroquois...and found a cosmological world that they believed to be far superior to the patriarchal one of the white nation in which they lived...."'

1995.034. Pietrie, H. M. [Letter to the Editor]. Anchorage (Alaska) *Daily News*. August 6, 1995, p. 4-J.

Pietrie is sketching a plan that will create "responsible, self-reliant communities...unified into a confederation for mutual trade, based on a sustainable economy." To govern these confederations, Pietrie suggests a model "based upon the Iriquois [*sic*] confederation system...[which] was copied by the early 'founders' of the United States...." Pietrie refers readers to Johansen, *Forgotten Founders* [1982].

1995.035. Porter, Robert B. "Strengthening Sovereignty Through Peacemaking -- The Seneca Nation's Experience." *Daybreak*, Vol. 1, No. 5 (1995), pp. 14-16.

Porter, attorney general of the Seneca Nation, examines an ongoing political crisis among the Senecas that has recently left three people dead, bringing into his case the history of the Iroquois. "This form of government," he writes, "served as the model for the American constitution, based on the notion that all human beings have the ability to use their minds and that all significant decisions should be reached by consensus." (p. 14)

1995.036. Saiz, Janet. "Treaty Opponents Ignore History" [letter to the editor]. Madison [Wisconsin] *State Journal*, March 22, 1995, p.9-A.

Saiz is replying to another letter in the paper by Diane Vaughan which asserts that Indian treaties are discriminatory. "As far as living by 'the same rules and laws as the rest of us,'" Saiz writes, "Most of the Constitution of 'our' founding fathers came from the laws of the Iroquois nation. Someone is badly in need of some real history lessons."

1995.037. Scott, Vernon. United Press International, Entertainment Desk, April 3, 1995.

Scott, UPI's Hollywood reporter, details the making of "500 Nations," the CBS television series financed and hosted by Kevin Costner, broadcast during 1995. The series is said to have been the brainchild of

Jack Leustig, who was asked in 1990 to make a half-hour documentary on the filming of "Dances With Wolves." Instead, Leustig convinced Costner to stake a nationally broadcast series on Native Americans. Leustig describes to Scott the genesis of the Iroquois Confederacy and its democratic attributes. The TV series includes a segment on the Iroquois which notes that the Iroquois model helped shape the founding of the United States.

1995.038. Shaw, Christopher. "A Theft of Spirit." *New Age Journal*, August, 1995, pp. 84-92.

The *New Age Journal* asks its audience whether plastic medicine men are ripping off Native American religious traditions for profit. In this context, author Shaw recalls his days as a youth in New York's Mohawk Valley. He briefly outlines the history of the Haudenosaunee, and the Great Law of Peace, adding, on page 87, "The law, which fosters the exercise of reason and clear thinking and protects free speech and equality for women, may have been influential in crafting the United States Constitution."

1995.039. Vesburgh, Lois. "Roles to Fill: South Dakota Researcher's Work, Performances Connect to CNY." Syracuse *Herald-American*, January 1, 1995.

This newspaper column describes performances of Matilda Joslyn Gage and Elizabeth Cady Stanton by Sally Roesch Wagner, who also has done considerable research into ways in which Iroquois political and social structures influenced their feminism. Wagner recounts Gage's surprise at finding that Iroquois women played important roles in political affairs at a time when women in the United States were property of their husbands and could not vote. "These women were amazed to learn that Native American women had rights long before white women in this country had them. The women in Iroquois tribes owned property and voted," Wagner is quoted as saying.

1995.040. West, Woody. "The Way West: Series' PC Myth-making Turns Indians Into Saints and Whites into Savages." Washington *Times*, May 7, 1995, p. D-1.

This is a review of several television productions dealing with American Indian History, including CBS' "500 Nations," Turner

Broadcasting's "The Native Americans," the Discovery Channel's "How the West Was Lost, and the PBS series "The Way West." The reviewer speculates that the outpouring of material sympathetic to Native Americans on national television is "a spasm of romanticism...blending sentimentalism, half-baked history, and soft-centered ideology." West quotes a review of the Turner series in the New York *Times*, "which scoffed at its assertion that Western democracy began with the Iroquois wampum belt [*sic*]: so much for John Locke."

Film and Video

1995.041. Video Tape, "America's Great Indian Nations," Quester Home Video (Chicago, Ill.).

This hour-long tape surveys the histories of the Iroquois, Seminole, Shawnee, Navajo, Cheyenne, and Lakota. Five times the script mentions the idea that the Iroquois political system helped shape democracy. The film briefly recounts the founding epic of the Iroquois and notes Benjamin Franklin's use of Iroquois concepts. Tape received from John Kahionhes Fadden (who contributed artwork to it) January 9, 1995.

1995.042. Kevin Costner's "500 Nations," an eight-hour documentary aired in four segments on CBS during the spring of 1995, contained references to Haudenosaunee government and Benjamin Franklin's use of its concepts. *TV Guide* (Vermont edition, supplied by John Kahionhes Fadden), provides a sketch of the show (on p. 71), which says that the segment to be aired May 27 shows "how the democratic Haudenosaunee inspired Ben Franklin to press for Colonial independence from England."

1994

Books, Scholarly and Specialty Journals

1994.001. Boyd, Doug. *Mad Bear: Spirit, Healing, and the Sacred in the Life of a Native American Medicine Man*. New York: Simon & Schuster/Touchstone, 1994.

"Influence" is mentioned on page 242 in the context of Native American contributions to general North American culture. On pages 262 and 263, Russell Means, who is quoted in a speech, paraphrases Benjamin Franklin's 1751 letter which encourages emulation of Iroquois governing methods ("It would be a strange thing if six nations...") Means says the statement was made at a meeting in 1746. He seems to be referring to the Albany Congress of 1754, at which Franklin proposed a plan combining British and Native American precedents.

1994.002. Caduto, Michael J. and Joseph Bruchac. *Keepers of Life: Discovering Plants Through Native American Stories and Earth Activities for Children.* Golden, Colo.: Fulcrum, 1994.

Page 8 briefly discusses the Iroquois use of a Great White Pine as a national symbol. On page 9, under a drawing of a Great White Pine by John Kahionhes Fadden, a caption observes that the Iroquois Tree of Peace [and the rest of the Iroquois political tradition] has helped inspire the United Nations Charter and the United States Constitution.

1994.003. Calloway, Colin G. *The World Turned Upside Down: Indian Voices From Early America.* Boston: Bedford Books/St. Martin's Press, 1994.

This book is part of the Bedford Series in History and Culture. It contains an excerpt from Cannassatego's 1744 speech at the Lancaster Treaty Council, at which he urged the colonists to unite on an Iroquois model. Comments the author: "Some people interpret Cannassatego's words as evidence that, forty-five years later, the Founding Fathers based the United States Constitution on that of the Iroquois."

1994.004. Champagne, Duane, ed. *The Native North American Almanac.* Detroit: Gale Research, 1994.

On pages 248 and 249, while describing Iroquois history and culture, this book provides a short overview of colonial-Native interaction, including advice by Iroquois leaders that the British colonies unite, as well as Benjamin Franklin's use of Iroquois precedents in the Albany Plan and Articles of Confederation. Comments by Jefferson and John Adams are included. *Exemplar of Liberty* [1991] is cited as a source.

Iroquois advice to the colonists is also included under "Cannassatego" and "Hendrick" in the biographical section of the *Almanac*.

1994.005. Champagne, Duane, ed. *Chronology of Native North American History*. Detroit: Gale Research, 1994.

An entry observing the birth of Hendrick (1680) on page 72 notes that his alliance with Anglo-americans helped shape United States political practices.

1994.006. Champagne, Duane, ed. *Native America: Portrait of the Peoples*. Detroit: Visible Ink Press, 1994.

On pages 61 and 62, this book briefly describes Iroquois contributions to the Albany Plan, as well as the writings of Thomas Jefferson and Tom Paine. Donald Grinde was a contributor to this book. The discussion of Iroquois contributions to democracy is illustrated with a drawing by John Kahionhes Fadden, depicting a ceremony at Independence Hall in 1776 during which a group of Iroquois sachems gave John Hancock an Onondaga name.

1994.007. Churchill, Ward. *Indians Are Us? Culture and Genocide in Native North America*. Monroe, Maine: Common Courage Press, 1994.

In "P is for Plagiarism," (pp. 167-172), Churchill argues that much of Jack Weatherford's *Indian Givers* was taken from Warren Lowes, *Indian Giver: A Legacy of North American Native Peoples* [1986], which includes a chapter titled "The Influence of Folk Democracy," outlining Iroquois contributions to the development of democracy. While Weatherford's general debt to Lowes' book is not known, on the "influence thesis," he also borrowed liberally (fairly, and with credit) from *Forgotten Founders* [1982, 1987]. The influence issue also arises in Churchill's review of Jerry Mander's *In the Absence of the Sacred* [1991]; Grinde, *The Iroquois and the Founding of the American Nation* [1977] is cited (pp. 147, 163).

1994.008. Gentry, Carole M., and Donald A. Grinde, Jr. *The Unheard Voices: American Indian Responses to the Columbian Quincentenary 1492-1992*. Los Angeles: American Indian Studies Center, 1994.

This record of a 1992 conference on Native Americans and the Columbus quincentenary at UCLA contains Bruce Johansen's essay on Roger Williams, reprinted from *Exemplar of Liberty* (1991).

1994.009. Grinde, Donald A., Jr. [Review of Gibson, John Arthur. *Concerning the* (Iroquois) *League.*] *American Indian Culture & Research Journal* 18:1(1994), pp. 175-177.

pp. 175-76: "Over the years, the League of the Iroquois has inspired the constitutional thought of founders such as Thomas Jefferson, Benjamin Franklin, and John Adams." Grinde writes that wider availability of this annotated text of the Iroquois Great Law of Peace in Onondaga and English will help increase understanding of Native American democratic practices. Gibson's is the first complete account of the Great Law in printed form. Orally, the Great Law takes roughly four eight-hours days to recite. A complete recitation is done every five years at Onondaga, near Syracuse, by Jacob Thomas.

1994.010. Grinde. "Teaching American Indian History: A Native American Voice." *American Historical Association Perspectives* 32:6 (September, 1994), pp. 1, 11-16.

A pointed debate between Grinde and James Axtell on the nature of historical scholarship, dominance and authority, and the likelihood that the Iroquois helped shape American democratic traditions. The debate, which takes place in the context of teaching standards for Native American history, includes a reply by Axtell and a rejoinder by Grinde in the December, 1994 edition of *Perspectives*, pp. 31-33.

1994.011. Haan, Richard. [Review of Lyons, *et al., Exiled in the Land of the Free.*] *The Journal of American History* 81:2 (Sept., 1994), pp. 641-642.

According to Haan, "There is not much new," in this book's assertion of Iroquois influence on the development of the democratic tradition. Haan surveys the eight essays in the book, and contends that the authors "fail to ask how much of the present-day Iroquois tradition of the Iroquois League has been influenced by contact with mainstream American culture."

1994.012. Hayden, Tom. "Running in Place: Pushing Past the Market in the Clinton Era..." *Tikkun*, January, 1994, p. 33.

Hayden, a founder of Students for a Democratic Society in the 1960s and a California state senator in the 1990s, invokes political decentralization as a way to dissemble the "special interest state." In *Tikkun*, a progressive Jewish journal, Hayden calls for a decentralization on "a Jeffersonian, or Quaker, or Iroquois" model in an economy based in an eco-system balanced for generations to come. A market-driven model is not adequate for such a future, writes Hayden. In politics, he says, "inspiration for such a vision can be taken from certain of the writings of Thomas Paine, Benjamin Franklin, and Thomas Jefferson, not to mention the Iroquois and other tribes that preceded the European arrival."

1994.013. Henry, William, III. *In Defense of Elitism.* Doubleday, 1994.

Henry is annoyed that the Heath anthology of American literature now "pointedly begins with Native American chants...rather than Pilgrim rhetoric." He also says that it is "wicked for the State of New York [to teach]... that one of the two main sources for the U. S. Constitution was the organizing pact of the Iroquois Indian nation." This statement appears to be based on the New York SED curriculum *Haudenosaunee: Past, Present, Future.*

1994.014. Jacobs, Wilbur. [Review of Lyons, *et al., Exiled in the Land of the Free* (1992).] *American Indian Culture & Research Journal* 18:1(1994), pp. 177-179.

Jacobs calls *Exiled in the Land of the Free* "a splendid new book" (p. 177), and observes that "Donald Grinde's penetrating analysis of Iroquois political theory stresses the impact of the Six Nations upon emerging American concepts of governance leading up to the Constitutional Convention....Non-Indian Iroquois researchers have consistently ignored the impact of Indian people upon the growth of American concepts of freedom and liberty." (pp. 178-179). Grinde's chapter was condensed from *Exemplar of Liberty* [1991].

1994.015. Jemison, G. Peter. "Setting the Record Straight," in Marta Moreno Vega and Cheryll Y. Greene, eds. *Voices From the Battlefront: Achieving Cultural Equity.* Trenton, N.J.: Africa World Press, 1994.

In this essay, part of a collection on multicultural themes, Jemison describes "the Indian roots of American democracy." He observes that Franklin, Rutledge, and Madison were among the Founders who were influenced by Iroquois democracy. "Strong counterforces were at work," Jemison says on page 26, to retain slavery and to favor some established interests, resulting in a Constitution that did not adhere strictly to Iroquois law, but contained vestiges of it.

1994.016. Johansen, Bruce E. [Review of Lyons, *et al.*, *Exiled in the Land of the Free* (1992)]. *American Historical Review*, 99:1(January, 1994) pp. 295-296.

1994.017. Josephy, Alvin, Jr. *500 Nations: An Illustrated History of North American Indians.* New York: Knopf, 1994.

On pages 50, 52 and 53, following a brief description of the Haudenosaunee (Iroquois) League, Josephy writes, "The confederacy envisioned by the Peacemaker...influenced enlightened seventeenth and eighteenth century philosophers and writers in the colonies and Europe who were seeking just ways for their people to be governed." Josephy says that Benjamin Franklin's Albany Plan of Union "drew inspiration" from the Iroquois League, and that its example had an "indirect influence" on debates during the Constitutional Convention in 1787. Josephy says that the way in which the two houses of the U.S. Congress use conference committees to reconcile differences resembles the procedures of the Iroquois League. This book was published in conjunction with a series on American Indians broadcast during 1995 by CBS News, hosted by Kevin Costner.

1994.018. Malone, John. *The Native American History Quiz Book.* New York: Quill/William Morrow, 1994.

On its back cover, the first question this books asks its readers is: "What confederation, first formed in 1570, had significant influence on the United States Constitution?" On page 76, this book also quotes from

Exemplar of Liberty (although it is not cited) regarding Thomas Jefferson's characterization of Indians' use of public opinion

1994.019. Patterson, Lotsee and Mary Ellen Snodgrass, *Indian Terms of the Americas.* Englewood, Colorado: Libraries Unlimited, 1994.

This is a short (270 pages) encyclopedia-type work covering North and South America. On page 113, under "Iroquois League," the authors outline the history and structure of the confederacy, then write: "The representative government of the league is thought by some historians to have been a model for the U.S. government's representative democracy."

1994.020. Quinn, Arthur. *New World: An Epic of Colonial America from the Founding of Jamestown to the Fall of Quebec.* Boston: Faber & Faber, 1994.

Quinn is a professor of rhetoric at the University of California. In this book, he outlines the founding legend of the Iroquois Confederacy and argues that it helped shape the United States. He presents events involving Benjamin Franklin and the Iroquois in some detail (pp. 450-452), beginning with Cannassatego's advice that the colonists unite on an Iroquois model in 1744. Quinn makes a point of the fact that Franklin publicized the Onondaga sachem's advice by printing the treaty on his press. Quinn also points out that Franklin's 1751 letter to his printing partner James Parker advising the colonists to unite as had the Iroquois was not private correspondence -- it was also published and publicized. "The Iroquois, strange to say, were not only providing the opportunity for this [colonial union]; they had long been providing by their example the method -- or so Franklin thought." (p. 450) Quinn says that the Iroquois model provided proof that a confederation need not result in the type of oppressive centralized authority that was much feared in the colonies. Since 1751, Franklin had been looking for a way to express his ideas for colonial union, and he found his forum in the Albany Congress of 1754.

1994.021. Reeve, Christina S. *Documents of Freedom: National School Celebration.* Costa-Mesa, California: Celebration U.S.A., 1994.

This booklet was a result of the second National School Celebration in 1992, which stressed America's patriotic heritage for several million elementary-school children. The 1992 celebration was a centenary for the first, held in 1892, for which the Pledge of Allegiance was written. The booklet contains an essay by Elizabeth Christensen ("Our Founding Grandfathers," pp. 36-37) observing Iroquois roots of American democracy; *Exemplar of Liberty* [Grinde and Johansen, 1991] is cited as a source. On p. iii, the book lists month-by-month themes for celebration. The theme for October is "How did the political and social order of Native Americans influence American democracy?"

1994.022. Stern, Kenneth S. *Loud Hawk: The United States Versus the American Indian Movement.* Norman: University of Oklahoma Press, 1994.

On pp. 227-228, as this book describes how Dennis Banks was given sanctuary by the Onondagas in the early 1980s, Stern observes that the Iroquois Confederacy's "government flowed from a constitution that was older than ours which was a model for both Benjamin Franklin and Karl Marx." Stern notes that the confederacy still operates. The book has no references, which is unusual for a university press publication.

1994.023. Suagee, Dean B. and Christopher T. Stearns. "Indigenous Self-government: Environmental Protection...A Tribal Review." *Colorado Journal of International Environmental Law and Policy*, Winter, 1994, pp. 59-104.

Page 67: "A number of scholars have shown that the social philosophers who are credited with creating these ideas [liberty and inalienable rights] and the founding fathers of the American republic...drew upon their knowledge of how the Indian nations of eastern North America governed themselves (especially...the Haudenosaunee). This piece points out that the founders did not emulate the Iroquois' notions of women's political influence. They cite *Forgotten Founders* [1982, 1987] and Jacobs, "How the Founding Fathers Ignored the Clan Mothers" [1991].

1994.024. Wallace, Paul A. W. *The White Roots of Peace: The Iroquois Book of Life.* Santa Fe, N.M.: Clear Light Publishers, 1994.

This is a reprint of Wallace's 1946 title with an original introduction by Tadadaho Leon Shenandoah, and Epilogue by Seneca historian John Mohawk. New artwork is also included from John Kahionhes Fadden, to whose family Wallace left the copyright after his death. For documentation of Wallace's references to Iroquois influence on the founding of United States fundamental law, see "Before 1975."

1994.025. Wunder, John R. *"Retained by the People:" A History of American Indians and the Bill of Rights.* New York: Oxford University Press, 1994.

On page 19, Wunder observes that "Recent scholarship argues that the Iroquois Confederation experience was on the minds of a number of delegates [to the Constitutional Convention] at Philadelphia, that several Constitutional Convention members who were in a position to shape the writing of the Constitution had observed the Six Nations republic." However, says Wunder, "Whatever amount of Iroquoian political theory was incorporated into the Constitution, the resulting document said little specifically about Native Americans." Wunder references Grinde, *The Iroquois and the Founding of the American Nation* [1977] and Johansen, *Forgotten Founders* [1982, 1987].

Trade Magazines, Newspapers and Specialty Journals

1994.026. Ahear, Lorraine. "Proposed Tribal Constitution Would Shift Power." Greensboro, N. C. *News & Record*, June 26, 1994, p. B-2.

This article discusses a proposed constitution for the Lumbees. It notes that some of its provisions are similar to the U.S. Constitution, "which was itself modelled after the tribal system of the Iroquois Indians of New York."

1994.027. Alexander, James. "Europeans, Not Indians, Gave Us Models for the Constitution." [Letter to the Editor] Washington *Times*, June 13, 1994, p. A-20.

Alexander, of Reston, Virginia, is replying to another letter to the editor, by Brian D. Brown (June 7), in which "he implies that our federal government is modelled after the Iroquois Confederacy." He follows with a number of valid European precedents, not sensing that both could have worked in tandem.

1994.028. Anquoe, Bunty. "President Offers Hope." *Indian Country Today*, May 4, 1994, pp. A-1, A-2.

This report on President Clinton's speech to tribal leaders on April 29 (see 1994: "Other Items") includes a passage on Native democracy. Quoting Clinton: "So much of who we are today comes from who you have been for a long time. Long before others came to these shores there were powerful and sophisticated cultures and societies here -- yours. Because of your ancestors, democracy existed here long before the Constitution was drafted and ratified."

1994.029. Bialczak, Mark. "Shenandoah Opens Woodstock With Call for Peace." Syracuse *Herald-Journal*, August 12, 1994, pp. A-1, C-5.

Jim Davis, environmental director of the Wittenberg Center, Bearsville, New York, is credited with bringing Oneida folksinger Joanne Shenandoah to the attention of organizers for the 1994 "Woodstock" music festival, a reprise of a similarly named event in 1969. Shenandoah opened the three-day event before about 250,000 people. Davis said that his group has been working to get an indigenous voice in such events, and that, "...Not enough people realize that Franklin and Jefferson started our democracy after studying the Iroquois model." Until about 1990, Shenandoah was a computer programmer; within a few years, she recorded several albums and became one of the best-known performers in Native America. She is married to Doug George Kanentiio. They live in Oneida Castle, New York, and operate Round Dance Productions, which preserves Iroquois arts.

1994.030. Callinan, Veronica. "Egocentric 'Crusade' Mentality Still Lives." [Letter to the editor] Toronto *Star*, March 5, 1994, p. B-3.

Callinan is replying to a letter published Feb. 26 by Dominic DiStasi of the Grand Orange Lodge of Canada, in which he asserts that Christian values are being "chopped away" because of changes in the prayer that is cited daily by members of the Canadian parliament. Callinan lists evidence of civilization by peoples who were not Christian, including "the democratic system of the Iroquois Confederacy that was used as a model for the United States constitution."

1994.031. Carman, John. "TBS Series Beats its Breast in Series on Indians." San Francisco *Chronicle*, October 10, 1994, p. E-1.

Carman, a television critic at the *Chronicle*, asserts that Ted Turner's series of American Indians is part of "a rush to overcompensate for past sins." Carman says that the segment "The Broken Chain," which aired on October 10, is "a visual dud combined with a verbal scold....For example, viewers are told flat out that the Founding Fathers based their understanding of liberty on Indian life -- no mention here of the Enlightenment or British political philosophy -- and modelled the first confederation of states after the Iroquois Confederacy."

1994.032. Chasing Bear, Oowah Nah. [Letter to the editor] The Indianapolis *News*, October 21, 1994, p. A-13.

Chasing Bear is replying to a negative review of Ted Turner's "The Native Americans." (see Garmel, Marion, below) "Heaven forbid that Ben Franklin was inspired by Iroquois nations to form the constitution of a fledgling nation! If Garmel [the reviewer] can tear herself away from the soap operas, she might learn that the U.S. Constitution follows Iroquois law, but what savage mind could possibly create so superior a way of life?" She concludes: "Garmel's ignorance is glaring, but she is not alone. After all, it's what the schools teach. The media reinforce it by continuous Hollywood portrayals. The racism is insulting. But then, I've heard it all before -- in the land of the free and the home of [Ted Turner's!] Braves."

1994.033. Clinton, William [President]. "Guest Essay." *Native Peoples.* 7:4(Summer, 1994), p. 5.

Excerpts from President Clinton's speech to Native leaders at the White House April 29, 1994, including: "So much of what we are today comes from who you have been for a long time. Long before others came to these shores, there were powerful and sophisticated cultures and societies here -- yours. Because of your ancestors, democracy existed here long before the Constitution was drafted and ratified."

1994.034. Garmel, Marion. "The Other Side of History: Ted Turner's Three Channels Focus on Native Americans." Indianapolis *News*, October 10, 1994, p. D-1.

Marion Garmel says that "there are people who would argue" with the Turner series' portrayal of Native Americans in "a kind of Eden where self-sufficient, highly organized tribes frolicked before the white man came to destroy their world." Some claims of the Turner series "may be suspect," wrote Garmel, "such as the idea that the Articles of Confederation came to the Founding Fathers from the example of 'the sea of Indian confederacies' that surrounded them." The quote is from *Exemplar of Liberty* [1991].

1994.035. George, Doug (Kanentiio). "Indian Reservations Have Reasons for Not Welcoming Anthropologists." Albany *Times Union*, November 15, 1994, p. A-14.

In a letter to the editor, George takes issue with statements attributed to Dean Snow, professor of anthropology at the State University of New York (Albany) in a feature article November 3 [See Karlin, Rick, below]. "It seems the anthropologists have once again managed to pick our bones for their own individual academic and economic gains," George writes. "We Iroquois have grown weary of having our culture, history and traditions taken apart by these social scientists. They have a nasty habit of treating us like bugs in a jar..."

On Snow's dismissal of the idea that the Iroquois' political system helped shape American democracy, George says, "While the anthropologists grudgingly concede that our people exercised a revolutionary influence on the world through our foods, technology and architecture, they illogically insist that we had little or no influence on the minds of the American colonists....Of course the authors of the U.S. Constitution were profoundly impressed by the democratic traditions of the Iroquois. Where else in the world could they have looked for examples of the free nation they were creating? Autocratic England? Dictatorial France? Serf-ridden Russia? Snow's rejoinder appeared in the letters column of the *Times Union* November 28. Calling George by his first name Snow disavowed any association with the "professionals who, according to George, "have intruded upon our ancient ceremonies, stolen our wampum belts and adamantly opposed the return of our sacred items." Snow maintains that he has great respect for the Iroquois, and that his recently published book, *The Iroquois*, shows this respect.

1994.036. Goodman, Walter. "A Romantic Tribute to the First Americans." New York *Times*, October 10, 1994, p. C-16[Cultural Desk].

In this review of Ted Turner's televised series "the Native Americans," Goodman faults "romantic pictures and expositions that mix fact with myth." One such mixture, writes Goodman, is "the view...[that] the political arrangements of the Iroquois Confederacy, a union of tribes in upper New York State, was a model for the framers of the United States Constitution. One Indian historian reports that the 'fundamental beginning of Western democracy as we know it' can be found in the Iroquois wampum belts. So much for John Locke."

1994.037. Hall, Steve. "Turner Series Shows Tribes' Side of History." Indianapolis *Star*, October 4, 1994, p. C-7.

"The documentary says that Native Americans gave Europeans such foods as potatoes, tomatoes, and corn, and even provided the framework for the U.S. Constitution in a 17th-century confederation of six Iroquois Indian nations in Upstate New York."

1994.038. Hopkins, John Christian. "Native Perspectives." Gannett News Service, June 30, 1994.

This article briefly surveys the American Revolution from a Native American perspective. It notes that the revolution caused a split in the Iroquois Confederacy, "whose constitution served as a model for the United States." Hopkins is a Narraganset who writes for the Norwich, Connecticut, *Bulletin*.

1994.039. Johnson, Nathan B. "Bulldozing the Religion of Indigenous Peoples." San Francisco *Chronicle*, July 22, 1994, p. A-23.

In this opinion piece, Johnson discusses the denial of constitutional protection for Native American religious practices, as well as the question of whether "industrialized society [can] recognize and integrate indigenous beliefs." Evidence suggests, writes Johnson, "that the highly democratic structures of the Iroquois Confederacy, including its multicameral legislature, had a strong influence on our founding fathers and the framework on the Constitution." [*Note*: the Iroquois Grand Council was unicameral, although its members comprised two groups -- older brothers and younger brothers -- which suggests a bicameral model. The Grand Council was not "multicameral."]

1994.040. Karlin, Rick. "Exploring Cures From the Iroquois...Author Shares Iroquois Discoveries." Albany *Times Union*, November 3, 1994.

This is a review of Dean Snow, *The Iroquois*, (Blackwell Publishers, 1994), which is described as "a sweeping narrative that traces the Iroquois culture from its beginnings a thousand years ago to its survival in today's United States and Canada." According to Karlin, Snow believes that the idea that the Iroquois influenced the patriots who drew up the U. S. Constitution is a "myth." Snow is a professor of anthropology at the State University of New York -- Albany.

1994.041. Kowinski, William S. "White by Birth, Indian by Choice..." Pittsburgh *Post-Gazette*, November 27, 1994, p. 6.

In this lengthy (4,370-word) piece on colonists who chose to live with Indians, the Iroquois League is described as a "...powerful confederacy whose intricate democratic system was studied by the Founding Fathers, and some elements incorporated into the U.S. Constitution."

1994.042. Leo, John. "On Society: The Junking of History." *U.S. News and World Report*, Feb. 28, 1994, p. 17.

In terms similar to his 1990 column "A Fringe History of the World," Leo assails beliefs of people he calls "Afrocentrists," as well as those who deny the Jewish holocaust, calling all "pure assertion [and] a growing contempt for the facts." He includes in his laundry list of attempts to "transform facts into opinion...the supposedly strong influence of Iroquois thought on the U.S. Constitution, now taught in many schools."

[Johansen's reply to Leo was published in *U.S. News & World Report*, April 18, 1994, p. 9. "We have a genuine need to factor the accomplishments of non-white people into our history..." In comparing advocates of Native American influence on American ideas to the debunkers of the Holocaust, writes Johansen, Leo "has the debilitating problem for a social critic of not being able to tell historical wheat from chaff."]

1994.043. Lipsyte, Robert. "Tonto: Onondaga Chief Oren Lyons, Native American..." *Esquire*, February, 1994, p. 39.

This lengthy article mentions Lyons' new book, *Exiled in the Land of the Free* [1992], and describes it as "an attempt to advance the historical scholarship of the Indian's impact on American democracy and the U.S. Constitution."

1994.044. Osborne, Lawrence. "Brutality and Chivalry in a Stormy New World." [Review of Arthur Quinn, *New World: An Epic of Colonial America*] *Newsday*, June 23, 1994, p. B-8.

Osborne writes that Quinn's portrayal of the Iroquois League's founding suffers from "sentimentalism." Osborne briefly describes the founding legend, and complains that Quinn portrays Deganawidah as "a kind of native Jesus." Osborne further complains that Quinn's assertions Iroquois statecraft's influence on the United States are "pretentious." Osborne says that the Iroquois were as brutal as other Indians, or the white colonists, and that Quinn has created a race of noble savages.

1994.045. Palazzetti, Agnes. "Officials to Close Reservation Bingo Hall..." Buffalo *News*, March 19, 1994, n.p.

At issue is an order to close a bingo hall on the Tuscarora Reservation in Lewiston, New York, by Anthony J. Hope, chairman of the National Indian Gaming Regulatory Commission. The bingo hall, opened the previous week by Joseph "Smokin' Joe" Anderson, was built without permission of the Tuscarora council of chiefs. In retaliation, Anderson and his allies formed their own council of chiefs. Timothy Toohey, a Lewiston attorney who has represented Seneca businessmen, is quoted as calling the traditional chiefs' denial of Anderson's bingo hall a dictatorial action. "Anderson can well make the argument that he and his supporters are part of the Tuscarora government," Toohey said. "He might remind the people in Washington that our Founding Fathers borrowed from the Iroquois Confederacy in forming our government. They borrowed its democracy. They did not borrow a dictatorship."

1994.046. Palmer, Louise. "Schools Feel Backlash to PC in Classrooms." Newhouse News Service, in Chicago *Sun-Times*, February 20, 1994, p. 36.

This piece is published in the news columns, but the author's point of view is evident *vis a vis* "politics insinuating its way into school curricula under the banner of 'multiculturalism,' 'environmentalism,' and 'diversity.'" An example of such, according to Palmer, is that in New York State, "11th-graders trace the roots of the U.S. Constitution to the practices of the Iroquois Native American tribes as well as the European Enlightenment." This statement is attributed to Diane Ravitch, probably from an earlier piece in the New York *Times* which quotes her. Palmer seems unaware that while such a curriculum was proposed in New York State and drafted by a team of Iroquois writers, it was not implemented because of opposition from the state's anthropological establishment.

1994.047. Reese, Charley. "Americans: Knowledge of Past is Key to Retaining Your Liberty." Orlando *Sentinel*, February 1, 1994, p. A-8.

Into the China shop that is the "influence" debate, like a bull, lumbers columnist Charley Reese, who says that ideas such as Iroquois influence on democracy lay a claim on gullible Americans because they don't know their own history. His version of history is simple: "All the institutions of American government are derived from our European culture. None comes from Africa or Asia or American Indians." Reese calls "ignorant" assertions in the recent Turner Broadcasting series "The First Americans" that "our forefathers derived the idea of the U.S. Constitution from the Iroquois Confederation." Reese is just getting warmed up. "It's not even worthy of comment, except to point out that only a person 100 per cent ignorant of American and European history could make such a dumb statement." Before leaving the scene, our bull leaves a 24-carat turd at the door: "The superbly educated authors of the American Revolution had nothing to learn from a primitive tribal alliance."

1994.048. Rheingold, Howard. "Singer On-line With Indian Culture." San Francisco *Examiner*, July 13, 1994, p. C-2.

The singer is Buffy Sainte-Marie; the story describes her efforts to educate Native American young people, especially using computer technology. One of the ideas she is promulgating is that Indians practiced ecology and consensus building a long time before both became popular among others. She says, "The Iroquois Confederacy used the kind of decentralized decision-making that modern 'network' organizations use today, just as the founding fathers of the United States borrowed key ideas from Iroquois statecraft when they framed the Constitution."

1994.049. Vann, Dee. "Here to Stay." [Letter to the editor] San Francisco *Chronicle*, August 6, 1994, p. A-20.

Vann, who lives in Pacifica, California, writes to express her appreciation of an article by Nathan B. Johnson, "Bulldozing the Religion of Indigenous Peoples." She adds: "There are those of us who are still refusing to believe that our Constitution was copied after the Iroquois Confederacy. How could that be -- these people are savages, heathens, the vanishing tribe? Well, don't you believe it. The American Indian is here to stay."

1994.050. Walters, Colin. "Excellent Arguments for Elitism...[Review of William Henry III, In *Defense of Elitism*, 1994] Washington *Times*, September 11, 1994, p. B-6.

Walters cites approvingly Henry's assertion that it is "wicked" for the State of New York to make the "influence" issue part of its public-school curriculum. Says Walters: "This intellectual debt was not, to say the least, profusely acknowledged by our Founding Fathers. It is a latter-day scholarly discovery (or should be say invention?), prompted by the same sort of special pleader who will tell you in the next breath how the pioneer white man hated, cheated, and murdered the red man, never finding anything of value in his culture."

1994.051. Waters, Harry F. "On the Trail of Tears." *Newsweek*, October 10, 1994, p. 56.

In this review of Ted Turner's "the First Americans," Waters takes issue with the film's assertion that the Iroquois helped shape democracy: "As an exercise in history, 'The Native Americans' may not escape scholarly challenge. For openers, its claim that the Iroquois confederacy provided the model for the U.S. Constitution will come as a revelation to those who thought the Magna Carta had something to do with it." Waters overstates the case to discredit it, a common tactic of opponents; the film asserts that the Iroquois provided *a* model, not *the* model. -- there is an enormous difference. In a similar vein, Waters seems not to fathom the possibility that the Iroquois and Magna Carta *both* could have had influence. His analysis seems to borrow from George Will, Richard Grenier, *et al.*

1994.052. Weiskind, Ida. "America's Storied History Worth Telling...Native American Tribal Structure Contributed Much to Our Constitution." Pittsburgh *Post-Gazette*, July 3, 1994.

"To their amazement, they [the founders] found that the Indians permitted free speech, free religion, and free assembly, and these freedoms formed the basis for our constitution." Weiskind briefly describes the Iroquois council's structure, and compares it with the U.S. Congress. This article appears to be written for children.

1994.053. Yoder, Edwin M. [Review of William Henry III, *In Defense of Elitism*, 1994]. Atlanta *Journal and Constitution*, October 9, 1994, p. N-8.

"I share Henry's annoyance that -- for instance -- the *Heath Anthology of American Literature* now 'pointedly begins with Native American chants...rather than Pilgrim rhetoric'.... I agree that it is 'wicked for the State of New York be taught that one of the two main sources for the U. S. Constitution was the organizing pact of the Iroquois Indian nation.' This is arrant nonsense." Yoder's is one of several responses to Iroquois influence on democracy which assume that the idea has no factual background. The reviewer thus mistakes his own ignorance for expertise on the subject.

Film and Video

1994.054. Film: "Kahnasatake [Oka]: 270 Years of Resistance," National Film Board of Canada, film maker Alanis Obomsawin.

This two-hour film chronicles the crisis at Oka, Quebec, which flared into violence during the summer of 1990. The film, which won an award as Best Canadian Film at the Toronto Film Festival (1993), describes Iroquois history and governmental structure, including an assertion that the Iroquois system "influenced the adoption of a democratic charter in North America."

1994.055. Transcript, "Talk Back Live," Cable News Network, October 28, 1994. (in LEXIS)

This talk show, which aired at 1 a.m. Eastern time, contained a segment in which Lynne Cheney, conservative director of the National Endowment for the Humanities under President George Bush, debated with Suzan Shown Harjo. The exchange covered a number of topics, one of which was assertion of Iroquois influence on the evolution of democracy. Harjo began the exchange: "I think it's awfully important to learn about the very great framers of the United States Constitution, who were...the Iroquois people, the Natchez people, the Muskogie people [who influenced] Benjamin Franklin, [George] Morgan, and Jefferson, [who] found camaraderie with...nations confederated for peacetime purposes. They didn't find that working model in Europe; they found it here with the native confederacies." Cheney replied: "It's not at all clear that this...is historically accurate. This is a hotly debated point."

Press Release

1994.056. "Trends in the News," Trends Research Institute [Rhinebeck, N. Y.] July 1, 1994. [in LEXIS].

The Trends Research Institute forecasts that, by the year 2005, American notions of patriotism will be refigured to include Native American traditions. "Laws also will reflect newly discovered elements of early Indian cultures. In fact, some of these elements, especially those of the Iroquois Confederacy, will experience a rebirth. Many Iroquois principles are said to have influenced the framers of the

Constitution more than 200 years ago." This forecast was composed by Gerald Celente, director of the Trends Research Institute.

1993

Books, Scholarly and Specialty Journals

1993.001.   Awiakta, Marilou.   *Selu: Seeking the Corn Mother*.   Golden, CO: Fulcrum, 1993.

This examination of Native American spirituality and feminism describes the Haudenosaunee (Iroquois) confederacy's political system and its influence on later concepts of democracy and feminism. Several times between p. 276 and the end of the book, Awiakta describes the impact on nineteenth-century feminism (citing Sally Roesch Wagner's work), and on democracy generally, citing Kickingbird [1987], Barreiro, ed. [1988], and Grinde and Johansen, *Exemplar of Liberty* [1991].

1993.002.   [Barreiro, Jose, ed.].   Book Review: *Indian Roots of American Democracy*. *Whole Earth Review*, No. 81 (December 22, 1993), p. 111.

1993.003.   Baldwin, J.   *"Green Delusions*: An Environmentalist Critique of Radical Environmentalism." *Whole Earth Review* 78 (March 22, 1993), p. 121.

Baldwin is reviewing (and, usually, fervently supporting the ideas in) Martin W. Lewis Green *Delusions* [1992], a case against what the author regards as environmental extremism. "To support the cause of direct democracy," comments Baldwin, "eco-radicals have sought out historical instances of its successful institution. Unable to hold up their own or their forebears' experimental efforts in communal living...they have turned instead to indigenous American social organization. One popular model of participatory democracy is the Iroquois Confederacy."   Baldwin retorts, paraphrasing Lewis in *Green Delusions*, "The Iroquois Confederacy is a particularly ill-considered exemplar. Admiring the Iroquois political system...for its democracy is like praising Nazi Germany for its enlightened forestry. The Five

Nations not only engaged in a highly successful campaign of ethnocide against their competitors in the fur trade, the Hurons, but they also raised the torture of war captives (those they chose not to adopt...) to an art."

1993.004. Brandao, J. A. [Review of *Exemplar of Liberty*, 1991]. *Canadian Historical Review* 74:3 (Fall, 1993), p. 436.

Brandao finds little merit in the assertions of *Exemplar of Liberty*; the reviewer's analysis closely resembles that of Elisabeth Tooker [1988, 1990], who is cited as an authority on the issue.

1993.005. Cheney, Lynne V. "Multiculturalism Done Right..." *Change*, January, 1993, p. 8.

Cheney, who headed the National Endowment for the Humanities, offers her "spin" on the debate over multicultural education. She, too, has picked up the Schlesinger assumption, possibly from William Starna, that New York State high school juniors are laboring over homework teaching them how the Enlightenment, the colonial experience in government, and the Iroquois Confederacy shaped the United States' founding. Such is, alas, not the case. Long before Cheney's article appeared, the Iroquois curriculum guide died, languishing in the bowels of a vacillating State Education Department which proposed to give final review to Trolls who had earlier condemned it. Of Iroquois contributions to democracy, Cheney says: "This is not an idea accepted by reputable historians." She compares the assertion of Iroquois contributions to democracy to the idea that "Egypt was a black nation."

1993.006. Gillespie, Sheena and Robert Singleton. *Across Cultures: A Reader for Writers*. Second Ed. Boston: Allyn and Bacon, 1993.

This English composition reader mentions the "influence thesis" twice. The first (p. 512), is in an introduction to "Hiawatha, the Great Unifier." The second, on p. 522, is in Ishmael Reed, "America: the Multicultural Society:" "Even the notion that North America is part of Western civilization because our government is derived from Europe is being challenged by Native American historians who say that the founding fathers, Benjamin Franklin especially, were actually influenced by the system of government that had been adopted by the Iroquois..."

1993.007. Grinde, Donald A., Jr. "The Iroquois and the Nature of American Government," *American Indian Culture and Research Journal* 17:1(1993), pp. 153-173.

This article, condensed from *Exemplar of Liberty* [1991], also was published in the spring, 1993 issue of *Historia*, the journal of the Polish Historical Association.

1993.008. Hughes, Robert. *Culture of Complaint: The Fraying of America.* New York: Oxford University Press, 1993.

Page 150: "American ideas of liberal democracy are only to be nourished at their sources, which lie absolutely within the European tradition; and it is far more important that the young should know about them before they go on to acquire whatever acquaintance they may wish to have with the ancient culture of the Dogon or the political institutions of the Iroquois." It is likely that the African Dogon know more about Hughes' culture than he does of theirs. David Maybury's *Millennium* [1992] contains a delightful account of a Dogon dance that includes an Anglo-american anthropologist figure.

1993.009. Interpress Service, comp. *Story Earth: Native Voices on the Environment.* San Francisco: Mercury House, 1993.

In this collection of statements on the environment from indigenous peoples around the world, Joseph Bruchac (Abenaki) recalls some of what he has learned from his people's neighbors, the Iroquois, including the structure of their Great Law of Peace. "That Great Law is now recognized by many historians as a direct influence on the formation of modern ideas of democracy and on the Constitution of the United States." (p. 6)

1993.010. Iron Thunderhorse. "Democracy: An Indian Legacy." *The Witness,* 76:4(April, 1993), pp. 26-27.

The Witness is published by the Episcopal Church Publishing Company, Detroit.

1993.011. Jacobs, Wilbur. "Columbus, Indians, and the Black Legend Hocus-Pocus." *American Indian Culture & Research Journal* 17:2(1993), pp. 175-187.

Jacobs maintains that the Iroquois were "great peacemakers as well as warriors." (p. 178). "We can learn much from the Indians' world-view of peacemaking and their concern for the welfare of future generations, as well as their ability to live together in harmony." (p. 184) "Perhaps the greatest debt America owes to Native American people is for our magnificent traditions of freedom and democracy. I scarcely need mention the volume *Exemplar of Liberty* by Donald A. Grinde and Bruce E. Johansen, which for the first time gives us widespread documentation of this indebtedness. Equally significant is the fact that the book is an exemplar of the fighting spirit in the front lines of knowledge, counteracting the cadre of well-meaning but misled scholars who call themselves 'Iroquoianists,' although the Iroquois themselves often decline to be identified with them. Against this formidable phalanx of academic shock troops, Grinde and Johansen have skillfully penetrated firing lines of generalities with barrages of understory factual research that toppled the opposition. Grinde and Johansen proved that the Indian people of North America left a legacy of freedom and democracy that is world-wide in its influence." (p. 184)

1993.012. Jacobs. Wilbur R. [Review of Barreiro, *Indian Roots of Democracy*, 1992]. *American Indian Culture & Research Journal* 17:2(1993), pp. 211-213.

Jacobs calls this book "an invaluable gift" (p. 211) to students of American Indian studies. He briefly reviews the contents of the book, the return of Iroquois wampum belts from the state of New York, and the debate over the "influence thesis," calling Prof. Elisabeth Tooker's arguments against Native American influence on democracy [1988, 1990] "speculative" and "weak on historical sources." (p. 212)

1993.013. Jennings, Francis. *The Founders of America.* New York: W. W. Norton, 1993.

The title of this trade treatment of Native American history nonwithstanding, Jennings is solidly against suggestions of Native American "influence" on democracy. On pages 186 and 187, Jennings writes that the Founders did not extend the protections of the Constitution to Indians. "In the seventeenth century [*sic*], protection for Indians was wholly inconceivable by the overseers of conquest (This thought should be noted by mythologists who assert that Indians strongly influenced the writers of the United States Constitution)." Jennings also assails the "myth" of the Albany Plan as forerunner of later political developments (p. 292), one of a number of "myths" that fall before his pen. Without naming any of them, or citing any of their work, Jennings enthusiastically squashes "mythologists" of several stripes elsewhere in this book, as well.

1993.014. Johansen and Grinde. "Native Voices and the Diffusion of an Idea." *Akwe:kon Journal* 10:2(Summer, 1993), pp. 30-39.

The authors survey the debate over assertions of a Native American role in the creation of democratic traditions in a framework of rhetorical analysis, finding that opponents of the "influence thesis" fall back on abuse of the principles of argumentation to conceal the lack of a factual basis for their argument. This article surveys support and opposition to the idea, mainly since late 1989, where their narrative is picked up in Johansen and Grinde, "A Recent Historiography," *American Indian Culture & Research Journal* 14:1 (1990). This article was reprinted in the Winter, 1994 edition of *Cultural Survival Quarterly*, pp. 24-28.

1993.015. Kawashima, Yasuhide. [Review of Grinde & Johansen, *Exemplar of Liberty*, 1991], *American Historical Review* 98:3(June, 1993), p. 941.

Kawashima finds *Exemplar of Liberty* to be "a challenging book," and "a penetrating study of how Native American nations practiced their democracy," with a "succinct portrayal" of Roger Williams' use of native precedents for political freedom and religious toleration. Kawashima says that Grinde and Johansen have "meticulously collected" historical information to build a case that Native American political institutions had an impact on the founding of the United States, but that the authors "seem overly zealous in claiming more than their evidence can substantiate....Many of their statements are overdrawn." The reviewer takes exception to *Exemplar's* tracing of feminism, the Northwest Ordinance, judicial review, and the Bill of Rights in part to Native American origins.   The question, says Kawashima, is no longer whether Native American precedents helped shape democracy, but to what extent.

1993.016. Knight, Margy Burns. *Who Belongs Here?   An American Story.* Tilbury, 1993.

This children's book (ages 8-12) describes the immigration of a Cambodian family to the United States, and is written as a social-studies unit on cultural diversity. Among a number of subjects, according to *Kirkus Reviews* [September 1, 1993], the book says that the Iroquois Great Law of Peace was used as a model for parts of the U.S. Constitution. The endnotes of the book say that such assertions are "speculative."

1993.017. Mancall, Peter C. [Review of *Exemplar of Liberty* (1991)]. *The Journal of American History*, June, 1993, p. 248.

While *Exemplar of Liberty* includes "occasional glimpses into a vibrant multicultural world," and provides "some fine examples" of the ways that colonists used American Indian symbols, Grinde and Johansen "read too much into such matters," in Mancall's opinion. He believes that "the central arguments of the book remain unconvincing."

1993.018. McSloy, Steven Paul.   "Back to the Future: Native American Sovereignty in the 21st Century." *Review of Law & Social Change*, Vol. 20(1993), pp. 218-300.

In a footnote (p. 221), McSloy mentions the debate over the "influence" issue as evidence that Native Americans had complex governments before contact with European law. He quotes from Franklin's 1751 letter to James Parker arguing for emulation of the Iroquois Confederacy in a colonial federation.

1993.019. Mikolajczyk, Waleria. "Poland and the American Indian: Friends of the Red Man." *The Warsaw Voice.* January 17, 1993.

This article describes the activities of the Polish Friendship Society, a group of Poles who study American Indian history and issues, publish books, and edit a journal. The group also organizes peaceful protests on behalf of Native American people and causes, such as freedom for Leonard Peltier. The publishing house, called Tipi, has issued about a half-dozen titles, and the journal, *Tawacin Quarterly*, has published since 1986. "The quarterly includes materials about the Great Peace Law, which is a discovery for the Polish reader. The law made it possible for the confederation of five Iroquois nations to function in harmony for several centuries. The editors stress that this law was taken by white colonists as a model for the United States constitution...and a model for democracy, but later the colonists forgot for long years both the Indian original and its authors."

1993.020. Miller, Robert J. "American Indian Influence on the United States Constitution and its Framers." *American Indian Law Review* 18(1993) pp. 133-160.

Miller, an adjunct professor of law at the Northwestern School of Law (Lewis and Clark College, Portland, Oregon) writes that "Native Americans played a significant role in shaping the United States Constitution, and had a profound impact on several of the Founding fathers..." The article provides a detailed description of attention paid to Native American themes by Franklin, Jefferson, Madison, and other Founders, citing Grinde [1977], Weatherford [1988], Johansen, [1982, 1987], and Cohen [1952].

1993.021. Morris, C. Patrick. "Who Are These Gentle People?" *American Indian Culture and Research Journal* 17:1(1993), pp. 1-15.

Morris, professor of liberal studies, University of Washington (Bothell), describes the first encounters between Columbus and the Tainos, whom Columbus described as "these gentle people." Morris then takes issue with the "narrow Eurocentric view of discovery and its aftermath" (p. 8). Morris cites Grinde's article in the same issue of *AICRJ* (above), and says (on page 8) that it "sets out evidence for substantive contributions by American Indians, particularly the Iroquois, to the form of federalism adopted by the United States through its Constitution. The academic debate precipitated by the injection of Indians into the authorship of this most precious of all United States historical documents is indicative of the intellectual climate surrounding scholarship related to Indians and other indigenous peoples. After 500 years, it is time we have this debate."

1993.022. National Geographic Society. *The World of the American Indian.* Washington, D.C.: National Geographic Society, 1993.

On page 133, this book gives a brief description of the Iroquois League and its creation, and then comments: "Our own nation's founding fathers knew about the Iroquois Confederacy and admired its effectiveness." Benjamin Franklin's 1751 letter to his printing partner James Parker ("It would be a strange thing if...") is quoted.

1993.023. Royal Commission on Aboriginal Peoples [Canada]. *Partners in Confederation: Aboriginal Peoples, Self-Government, and the Constitution.* Ottawa: Government of Canada, 1993.

This report considers alternatives to Canada's present confederation, and Native American peoples' roles in Canadian governance. Iroquois models of government are presented, and *Exemplar of Liberty* [1991] is cited. The report argues that the Canadian confederation has come more to resemble the Iroquois League over time, moving gradually from exclusive reliance on its British origins.

1993.024. Utter, Jack. *American Indians: Answers to Today's Questions.* Lake Ann, Mich.: National Woodlands Publishing Co., 1993.

Most of this book is in question-and-answer format. Under the question "Who are the Six Nations?" on pages 42 and 43, Utter provides a brief description of the Iroquois League and its Great Law of Peace, and compares its structure to that of the United Nations. Utter also writes that "In the mid-1700s, the sophisticated political organization and powerful confederacy of the Iroquois strongly impressed several future revolutionaries like Benjamin Franklin and others...[who]...borrowed at least some of their ideas from experiences with the Iroquois. Grinde [1977] and Johansen [1982] are referenced. In an appendix, on pages 295-296, the book reproduces the U. S. House of Representatives resolution acknowledging Iroquois contributions to democracy.

1993.025. Waters, Frank. *Brave Are My People: Indian Heroes Not Forgotten.* Santa Fe: Clear Light Publishers, 1993.

In his capsule biography of Deganawidah, the Peacemaker, Waters writes (p. 7) that "the Peacemaker...had a dream: a wonderful, practical dream that came true for all America." At the end of the sketch, he elaborates, on pp. 12-13: "The influence of the League of the Iroquois upon the course of this nation, the United States of America, has been in the highest degree. For it is believed now that because the framers of the Constitution were familiar with the League, the charter for the government of the United States was modelled upon many of its principles. Whether or not this is true, the symbols of the great pine and the eagle, and the concept of a number of separate peoples united in a federation for the good of all, were derived from American roots and given practical expression through the Peacemaker and Hiawatha."

Newspapers, Magazines, and Newsletters

1993.026. _____. "Choosing New Iroquois Representatives." Business Wire, July 12, 1993 [in LEXIS].

Datelined Syracuse, this press release begins: "Despite the fact that much cf the U.S. form of government is based on the Iroquois Confederacy, the U.S. democratic system did not adopt the Iroquois idea of total consensus." A brief description of traditional Iroquois decision-making follows. The release lists as author "Loretta V. Metoxen, Native American News," with a telephone number, [800] 236-2214.

1993.027. _____. "Native Americans and the Birth of Democracy." [Book review of Lyons, *et al.*, *Exiled in the Land of the Free*, 1992.] February 21, 1993, St. Louis *Post-Dispatch Everyday Magazine*, p. 5-C.

"Growing evidence indicates that the Constitution, the Bill of Rights, and other significant influences on the fundamental philosophical base of American democracy can be traced to indigenous roots." The review is favorable.

1993.028. _____. "Who 'Invented' Democracy? July 2 Events Honor Native Americans." Aspen [Colorado] *Times Daily*, July 1, 1993, p. 10.

This article describes a series of events regarding Native American contributions to democracy planned by Sarah Pletts of Aspen's Living Arts Foundation for July 2.

1993.029. _____. "A Curriculum Guide to Learning About Native Americans." *Tekawitha Newsletter* (Great Falls, Montana), March-April, 1993, p. 4.

This brief survey of American Indian contributions to our material life and ideas cites Benjamin Franklin's debt to the Iroquois for the concept of a loose federation of states.

1993.030. _____. "Multicultural Law a Weapon For Indoctrination by Zealots." Omaha *World-Herald*, September 26, 1993, p. 12-B.

This lead editorial, by Frank Partsch (editor of the *World-Herald's* editorial pages), takes issue with a new state law mandating multicultural education, disagreing at length with comments by George Garrison (below) reported in the *World-Herald* a week earlier. Partsch admits that Franklin and Jefferson had many contacts with Native Americans and wrote approvingly of their cultures, but believes that the case for Native American contributions to democracy is "overstated." Partsch cites a comment by Francis Jennings, senior research fellow at the Newberry Library, that Indians were excluded from the protections of the U.S. Constitution: "This thought....should be noted by the mythologists who insist that Indians strongly influenced the writers of the United States Constitution." [see Jennings, above] A response by Garrison was published September 30, followed by a response by Johansen October 8, which was paired with a rebuttal to Garrison by another author.

1993.031. Alia, V. [Review, Lyons, *et al.*, *Exiled in the Land of the Free*(1992)]. *CHOICE*, vol. 30, No. 9 (May, 1993), p. 1535.

"Every library should have this important challenge to the still-prevalent ethnocentrism in histories of American democracy," writes the reviewer, who also faults the eight male co-authors of *Exiled* because the role of women is "largely absent" from the book. *Exiled*, says Alia, "clarifies Native American influences on U.S. political structures."

1993.032. Associated Press. "Multicultural Law Misunderstood, Educator Says." Omaha *World-Herald*, September 19, 1993.

George Garrison, chair of black studies at the University of Nebraska at Omaha, is quoted at a meeting in Norfolk, Nebraska, regarding the state's new multicultural-education law. "Many history courses also teach that the principles of democracy were founded on the beliefs of Europeans, such as John Locke, Garrison said. While multiculturalism does not attempt to discredit those contributions, it also recognizes that many of the ideas presented at the Continental Congress also came from American Indians."

1993.033. Casey, Constance. "The Thinking Man's Rush Limbaugh." Los Angeles *Times*, May 23, 1993, Book Review Section, p. 10.

Casey is reviewing two books, Robert Hughes' *Culture of Complaint: the Fraying of America*, and Rush Limbaugh's *The Way Things Ought to Be*. "These two books, in reaction to political correctness and multiculturalism, appear on the best-seller lists this week." She asserts that while their writing styles are very different, Hughes and Limbaugh are "brothers under the skin." One area in which they agree, writes Casey, is "they both...deny that the Iroquois had any influence on the Constitution."

1993.034. Dawson, Greg. "Turner Retells the Story of Indians..." Orlando *Sentinel*, December 5, 1993, p. D-1.

This review of Turner's "The Broken Chain" says: "It recounts a fascinating chapter of American Indian history surely unfamiliar to most viewers -- the story of the Iroquois Confederacy, a sophisticated organization of six Indian nations in the Northeast that became a model for the U.S. Constitution." Dawson notes that the founders failed to observe the power of clan mothers in the confederacy, and did not include Iroquois-style women's rights in the Constitution.

1993.035. Durling-Jones, Voyce. "A Paradigm Shift in the Americas: Biopolitics and Bioeconomics." *Tekawennake* [Brantford, Ontario], July 7, 1993, pp. 5, 14.

Durling-Jones is a member of the Canadian diplomatic corps, most recently consul general to Liberia. This is a transcript of a speech he gave in Vancouver, B.C., "Doing Business With Aboriginal Canada." The speech mentions several Native American contributions to general North American culture, including "In the United States, the Iroquois Confederacy served as a model for the new colonial government's federal system -- paradigm shift -- though the true history of the Americas has still not been truly comprehended or proper acknowledgement yet given to the First Peoples of the Americas...."

1993.036. Ergo, David. "Our Debt to the Iroquois." [Letter to the editor], San Francisco *Chronicle*, October 16, 1993, p. A-20.

Ergo, of Palo Alto, cites Jack Weatherford's *Indian Givers*, in which "he shows, in great detail, how our founding fathers, especially Franklin, used the Great Law of the Iroquois in creating our democratic form of government -- using it not just as a broad outline, but as a model for many specific provisions in our Constitution."

1993.037. Feran, Tom. "'Geronimo Fits in With Turner's Vision: Cable Magnate Wants to Make a 'Roots' for Indians." Cleveland *Plain Dealer*, December 5, 1993, p. 10-11.

Feran is reviewing the second segment of Turner's "The Native Americans," which he describes as "built around the story of the Iroquois League of Nations...whose sophisticated political structure helped inspire the U.S. Constitution...and the Legend of the Peacekeeper [he means 'Peacemaker']."

1993.038. Freeman, John. "'The Broken Chain' is Honorable, but Devoid of Passion." San Diego *Union-Tribune*, December 12, 1993, p. 8, TV Week.

Freeman says that Ted Turner, "the Mouth of the South," is spending $60 million "to raise awareness of Indian history and culture." "To its credit," remarks Freeman, "'The Broken Chain does portray Iroquois as thoughtful and peace-loving -- until provoked. But once they're provoked, watch out! The movie also carries this important message: that the U.S. Constitution is based on the Iroquois tenet of many diverse nation-states being bound together as one nation."

1993.039. George, Doug (Kanentiio). "Mohawk Teacher Dispels Myths." Syracuse *Herald-American*, October 3, 1993, n.p.

This summary of Native American contributions to American culture salutes Ray Fadden. George observes: "Only secondary attention has been given to the diplomatic accomplishments of the Iroquois Confederacy, a union of sovereign states that had a profound impact on the government of the infant United States."

1993.040. Gould, James Jay. "*Green Delusions*: An Environmentalist Critique of Radical Environmentalism." *The Progressive* 57:3 (March, 1993), p. 39.

Gould is reviewing Martin W. Lewis' *Green Delusions*, which he characterizes as "a primer in eco-extremism:" "Lewis uses a similar example to question the eco-radicals' call for decentralization. He reminds us that while the Iroquois Confederacy is held up as a successful example of small-scale participatory democracy, the tribal confederacy also carried out an effective campaign of ethnocide against the Hurons to ensure a fur-trade monopoly."

1993.041. Hepworth, James K. "We Missed a Chance to Make a Point." Lewiston [Idaho] *Morning Tribune*, November 6, 1993, p. 30.

Hepworth cites Jack Weatherford's *Indian Givers* [1988] as he lists material and intellectual contributions of American Indians to mainstream American life. He says that "Weatherford points out just how heavily indebted our system of government is to the founding Indian fathers." Most of Weatherford's information in *Indian Givers* is from *Forgotten Founders* [1982, 1987]. "...The American federal system...as early students of Indian societies like George Washington and Benjamin Franklin could attest, derives not from Europe, as too many historians still mistakenly insist, but from Indian tribal organizations."

1993.042. Hodgson, Godfrey. "The Smelting Nation." [Review of Schlesinger, *Disuniting America*] *The Independent* [London, England], January 11, 1993, p. 23.

This reviewer picks up from Schlesinger's book the bit of creative assumption that students in New York State high schools are being taught that three factors influenced the U.S. Constitution: Enlightenment thought, the colonial experience in government, and the Iroquois Confederacy. This phrasing is taken from a draft of the Iroquois curriculum guide that was never implemented by the state, and thus not mandated in the state's schools. [It is amazing to watch the material from this draft become assumed "fact" in so many horror stories of "political correctness."]

1993.043. Holsopple, Barbara. "Ted Turner Revisits Indian History, Starting With Geronimo, Iroquois." Phoenix *Gazette*, December 3, 1993, p. 26.

This review of "The Broken Chain" briefly describes the Iroquois' "remarkably sophisticated political structure that is believed to be the basis for the [U.S.] Constitution." Holsopple points out that Founders did not adopt the power of women held by clan mothers in the Iroquois Confederacy.

1993.044. Holston, Noel. "TNT Indian Shows Are a Fine Start." Minneapolis *Star-Tribune*, December 5, 1993, p. 1-F.

Holston, a *Star-Tribune* staff reporter, criticizes Ted Turner for producing "the most ambitious TV project ever attempted about Indians" even as his Atlanta Braves urge their fans to use the "tomahawk chop" that many Native Americans find demeaning. He applauds the series, including "The Broken Chain," the segment that describes Iroquois history. "The Iroquois League...served as model for the founding fathers of the United States. In at least one important respect, however, the Iroquois nations were much more advanced: women were not shut of of their democratic decision-making."

1993.045. Howell, Peter. "Rock-Rap Rage Hammers at 'Elitist Wall.'" Toronto *Star*, January 14, 1993.

Entertainment writer Howell describes the stage act and thoughts of vocalist/lyricist Zack de la Rocha, lead singer of Rage Against the Machine, "a powerful new hardcore rock and rap band coming Sunday to the Opera House." According to Howell, the band "weld rock and rap together to make brutally beautiful music that demands a reaction from the audience." During one cut, "Take the Power Back," the band peppers an American flag with "hot lead." As for present-day America, de la Rocha, who is of mixed Mexican and German heritage, says, "It is a machine that will do anything to keep going. It has no moral understanding or any true sense of the word 'freedom,' or 'democracy.' The only true democracy ever experienced throughout the Americas was the one the Iroquois Indians had."

1993.046. Hum, Debbie. "Ottawa Has No Right to Impose its Law on Natives: Mohawk." Montreal *Gazette*, March 18, 1993, p. A-5.

Stuart Myiow, Sr., a Kahnawake Mohawk elder, criticized a statement by Bertha Wilson, a retired Supreme Court justice who is a member of the Royal Commission on Aboriginal Peoples. Wilson had said that Canada can impose its laws on aboriginal people within its borders. Myiow replied: "We [Mohawks] have a great law, a constitution, which you people have taken from us. You have no right to legislate any laws over our people...Our lands are not yours to be assumed. You are my tenant, whether you like it or not."

1993.047. Johansen, Bruce. "Defending Multiculturalism." Omaha *World-Herald*, Oct. 8, 1993.

Response to Omaha *World-Herald* editorial (above), "Multicultural Law a Weapon for Indoctrination by Zealots," which was written after University of Nebraska at Omaha Black Studies Director George

Garrison was reported to have advocated more attention to multicultural education, including Iroquois influence on democracy, at a meeting in Norfolk, Nebraska.

1993.048. Johns, Donald. "Native Roots: How the Indians Enriched America." *Whole Earth Review*, December 22, 1993, p. 110.

Johns reviews Jack Weatherford's *Native Roots*, noting that he describes the Native American origins of 2,000 words in our daily speech (for those of us who speak American English), as well as government (the Iroquois model of democracy); he observes that half our food crops also come from Indians. Such things "ought to be the stuff of school curricula," remarks Johns.

1993.049. Jones, Jeff. "Capitol Intensive: Indian Guide." *Metroland* [Albany, N.Y.], January 28, 1993.

Jones surveys the latest flareup in the four-year-old controversy over the New York State curriculum guide *Haudenosaunee: Past, Present, Future*, a Native-composed section of the New York State Department of Education's "Curriculum of Inclusion," which has become a flashpoint in the national debate over multiculturalism. Jones summarizes Prof. William Starna's criticism of the guide, and other scholars', as well as Iroquois, replies: "Jack Wandell, an Albany writer and filmmaker and long-time supporter of the traditional Iroquois chiefs, [said] 'I see it [Starna's critique] as an escalation of the old-boy, mainly white network to shore up their entrenched advocacy of being the only ones who are in the know about Indians.'" After he heard that Governor Mario Cuomo had saluted Iroquois contributions to democracy in one of his speeches, Starna is reported to have "hit the roof." Starna has urged that such references be removed from the *Haudenosaunee* guide. [Files contain copious correspondence between Profs. Johansen, Grinde, Sally Roesch Wagner, Robert W. Venables and Bruce A. Burton, as well as John Kahionhes Fadden, as they formulated a collective reply to Starna, dated Feb. 12, 1993.]

1993.050. LaLonde, Michelle. "Mohawks Express Great Hope for Aboriginal Royal Commission." Montreal *Gazette*, May 4, 1993.

Mohawks at Akwesasne are reported to "have respect...and expect results from" the recently appointed Royal Commission on Aboriginal Peoples. "In another display of respect for the commission," reports LaLonde, Mohawk traditional subchief Jake Swamp gave them a condensed two-hour oral version of the Great Law of Peace, "which Mohawks say spawned western democracy and the U.S. Constitution." This piece also describes the historical significance of the Two Row Wampum, and the right of clan mothers to impeach errant chiefs.

1993.051. LeMay, Konnie. "Native Actors Shine in TNT's 'The Broken Chain.'" *Indian Country Today*, December 22, 1993, pp. A-1, A-2.

Page A-2: "The film depicts a discussion among the founding fathers of the United States about the democratic methods employed by the [Iroquois] Confederacy and how that influenced the government[al] structure the Americans would adopt. As Joseph Brant said in the film: The United States is 'a nation that was created in our image and with the blood of the Iroquois people.'"

1993.052. Leonard, John. "The Broken Chain." [Television review] *New York Magazine*, December 13, 1993, p. 94.

Leonard is reviewing Ted Turner's series "The Native Americans." He finds the second segment, "The Broken Chain" "as pedestrian as last week's 'Geronimo'." Leonard observes that "...the American revolutionaries...are no more bound by their treaties with these noble savages than their colonial oppressors, even though they borrow Iroquois principles to make their Constitution shipshape."

1993.053. Lipsyte, Robert. "Lacrosse: A Goalie Keeps Faith for an Iroquois Nation." New York Times, January 29, 1993, p. B-14 [Sports].

This is a feature on Oren Lyons, faithkeeper of the Onondagas, as a lacrosse player (he is in the Syracuse Sports Hall of Fame). Lyons says that when he was a young man (he was 62 in 1993), there were three ways an Iroquois could prove his manhood -- high steel, the Army, and lacrosse. Lipsyte also says that Lyons has just authored *Exiled in the*

Land of the Free [1992] which "maintains that most of the best aspects of American democracy were strongly influenced by Indian culture."

1993.054. Miller, John J., "The Moonbeam of Self-Esteem." *Newsday,* June 2, 1993, p. 84.

Miller, who is associate director of the Manhattan Institute's Center for the New American Community, decries attempts to build minority students' self-esteem with "pride-building curricula," or "pumping them full of stories meant to inflate racial pride." Two examples of this occur when "schools portray them of the rightful inheritors of the black scholars in ancient Egypt...or the Iroquois political theorists who inspired the Founding Fathers to write the Constitution."

1993.055. Rayl, A.J.S. "New Technologies, Ancient Cultures..." *Omni,* August, 1993, p. 46.

This wide-ranging piece describes attempts by Native Americans to preserve sovereignty and culture with technological tools such as computers and remote broadcasting. Along the way, the author observes that "essential principles" in the U.S. Constitution are borrowed from the Iroquois Great Law of Peace. Even as they borrowed Indian political structure, the colonists plundered the native peoples and their lands, Rayl writes.

1993.056. Rheingold, Howard L. "Indian Roots of American Democracy." *Whole Earth Review,* December 22, 1993, p. 111.

This is a review of Jose Barreiro, ed., *Indian Roots of American Democracy.* Rheingold observes at the beginning of his review that the Iroquois "social contract -- the Great Law of Peace -- almost certainly informed the creators of the U.S. Constitution." Rheingold details Benjamin Franklin's experiences among the Iroquois and his construction of the Albany Plan of 1754. Quoting Julian Boyd, editor of Jefferson's papers, Rheingold then links the Albany Plan to the later Articles of Confederation and Constitution. The reviewer also observes that in 1775 Colonial delegates thanked the Iroquois for Cannassatego's advice on national union in 1744.

1993.057. Seligman, Daniel. "Measuring PC: Those Influential Iroquois..." *Fortune*, April 19, 1993, p. 159.

In his column "Keeping Up," Seligman takes aim at "political correctness," which he describes as "a movement driven by truly totalitarian impulses, [which] is embodied in thought police who endlessly endeavor to suppress data..." Seligman then hauls the issue of Iroquois influence on the Constitution out as his primary exhibit of "politically correct" thought, which Seligman links to a general decline in American educational levels illustrated by a purported decline in Scholastic Aptitude Test results. He calls assertions of influence "fatuous," and quotes Schlesinger in *Disuniting of America* [1992]. Seligman's critique may be cribbed from a number of other conservative critics of the "influence" idea who disparaged it before him.

1993.058. Smolla, Rodney A. "Last in War, Peace, and the Supreme Court." *New York Times Book Review*, April 11, 1993, p. 22.

In this review of Oren Lyons, *et al.*, *Exiled in the Land of the Free* [1992], Prof. Smolla says that the book "explores the relationship of Indians to the Constitution from two directions....First, how Indian traditions may have influenced the creation of the Constitution, and second, how subsequent interpretations of the Constitution have affected the lives of Indians over time." On the subject of influence, Smolla, who is director of the Institute of Bill of Rights Law at the College of William and Mary, writes that the book makes a good case for Iroquois influence on the Constitution from the Albany Congress (1754) through the Philadelphia Convention in 1787, that Benjamin Franklin and other Founders were students of the Iroquois as well as of other political systems, and that European philosophers such as Locke and Rousseau also drew upon native precedents. Smolla writes that "[T]he authors make a compelling case for the existence of an Indian civilization of participatory democracy rich in its respect for individual human dignity, yet steeped in values of community."

In the same issue of the *Book Review*, on page 1 [Linda Bradley Salamon, "When Nobody Reasons Together"], the influence issue is mentioned in the context of a review of two books [Robert Hughes. *The Culture of Complaint: The Fraying of America*. New York: New York

Public Library/Oxford University Press, 1993; Jonathan Rauch. *Kindly Inquisitors: The New Attacks on Free Thought.*

1993.059. Tooker, Elisabeth. [Review of *Exemplar of Liberty* (1991)]. *Northeast Anthropologist* 46(Fall, 1993), pp. 103-107.

1993.060. Weintraub, David. "Iroquois Influence in the Founding of the American Nation." *Court Review* 29 (Winter, 1992) pp. 17-32.

1993.061. Will, George. "'Compassion' on Campus." *Newsweek*, May 31, 1993, p. 66.

In terms similar to those used in his syndicated columns [1989, 1991], Will lambasts new explorations in African and Native American history: "Religious fundamentalists try to compel 'equal time' in school curricula for creationism and evolution. But they are less of a threat than liberals trying to maintain 'fairness' for dotty ideas that make some 'victim groups' feel good -- ideas such as that Greek Culture came from Black Africa [an allusion to Martin Bernal's *Black Athena*], or that Iroquois ideas were important to the making of the Constitution."

1993.062. Zoglin, Richard. "Ted Turner Goes Native." *Time*, December 6, 1993.

In this review of the Turner Network series of television movies on Native Americans, Zoglin comments that in the segment "The Broken Chain," which began broadcasting December 12, 1993, "The acting is more wooden and the drama more sketchy than in *Geronimo* [The TV movie broadcast on TNT December 5]. Yet the history lesson -- that principles of the Iroquois Confederacy were an important influence on the American Constitution -- is well told."

Video

1993.063. Transcript #863, "Independence Day: Our Indian Legacy," *Larry King Live,* Cable News Network, July 5, 1993.

With Pat Mitchell sitting in for Larry King, the show observed Independence Day by inviting Oren Lyons to talk about Native American precedents for United States fundamental law. Lyons described Iroquois consensus-making practices, the story of the Peacemaker, and colonists' early encounters with Native Americans that provided channels of communication for Native American ideas. Lyons also described the contents of his new book *Exiled in the Land of the Free* [1992]. Lyons described one student of his in Buffalo who was "very angry" because, at age 32, with four children, he had never been told of the Iroquois influence on U.S. fundamental law. "My children are going to hear about this," Lyons quotes the student as having said. Lyons also answered calls from the audience about "influence" assertions. One caller stressed the importance of women in the Iroquois political system. Lyons thanked the caller, and described ways in which Iroquois clan mothers nominate leaders in the confederacy.

1992

Books, Scholarly and Specialty Journals

1992.001. _____. [Review of Oren Lyons, *et al.*, *Exiled in the Land of the Free* (1992)] *Publisher's Weekly*, September 14, 1992, p. 92.

"These impressive essays by eight Native American leaders and scholars present persuasive evidence that the American colonists and the U.S. founding fathers borrowed from the Iroquois Confederacy and other Indian political institutions in drafting the U.S. Constitution."

1992.002. Altherr, Thomas. [Review, Weatherford, *Indian Givers*, 1988.] *American Indian Quarterly*, Spring, 1992.

Weatherford's first of two trade books on Native American influences devotes three chapters to political factors, some of it cited from *Forgotten Founders* [1982, 1987]. Altherr: "The next three chapters dip us into politics.... [Weatherford] underscore[s] a claim that these tribal peoples developed the concept of liberty...." Altherr criticizes Weatherford's analysis as too simplistic, and says he "would have profited enormously from reading Elisabeth Tooker's and Bruce Johansen's exchange on the subject in 1988 and 1990 volumes of

Ethnohistory." Altherr had forgotten that in a book published in 1988, Weatherford could have had no knowledge of the *Ethnohistory* articles.

1992.003. Axtell, James. *Beyond 1492: Encounters in Colonial North America*. New York: Oxford University Press, 1992.

Pages 285-286: Axtell notes that "early Quincentennial issues of the *Northeast Indian Quarterly* were devoted to 'Indian Roots of American Democracy' and 'Indian Corn of the Americas: A Gift to the World.' These subjects are typical of the 'contributions' approach that has been a dominant theme of Native American Studies since their [*sic*] inception in the late '60s, a phrase that all minority studies tend to go through on their way to cultural assurance and self-definition." Axtell believes that such studies "marginalize their own group by making it conform or 'contribute' to the dominant culture and its standards of importance, rather than assert the integrity and value of their own cultures and histories." "Thus far," writes Axtell, "the discussion of the native contribution to American democracy has been limited to the alleged Iroquois influence on the Founding Fathers, though in *Indian Givers* and *Native Roots*, anthropologist Jack Weatherford seeks to describe, in the words of his subtitles, *How the Indians of the Americas Transformed the World*, and *How the Indian Enriched America*."

1992.004. Bardes, Barbara, *et al*. *American Government and Politics Today: The Essentials*. West Publishing Co., 1992.

In the 1992-1993 edition of this introductory political science textbook for college students, a box on page 66 asks: "Did you know...that the federal government of the United States was modeled, in part, on the sixteenth-century Iroquois Confederacy...?" On page 140, in a larger box titled "The Iroquois Confederacy and American Democratic Principles," the idea is developed in more detail. The source is listed as "Jerry Stubben, Iowa State University." Stubben, professor of political science at Iowa State who is part Ponca, appeared on a 1991 Organization of American Historians panel with Grinde and Johansen, and exchanged information with them. In the 1994-1995 edition of the book, all references to the Iroquois and democracy were excised.

1992.005. Barreiro, Jose, ed. *Indian Roots of American Democracy*. Ithaca, N.Y.: Akwe:kon Press/Cornell University, 1992.

This collection of essays on the "influence" issue contains some from the earlier volume by the same name [see Barreiro, ed., 1988]. This volume adds updated material from *Akwe:kon Journal*(*Northeast Indian Quarterly*) by Venables, Wagner, *et al.* The introduction, by Jose Barreiro, contains an analysis of the "influence" debate to 1992.

1992.006. Berman, Paul, ed. *Debating P.C.: The Controversy Over Political Correctness*. New York: Laurel Books/Dell, 1992.

Diane Ravitch contributes an essay to this book that opposes the "influence" idea. Reviewing the book in The New York *Times*, Frank Kermode comments: "...Ms. Ravitch is wrong to deny the influence of the Iroquois (Haudenosaunee) in Upstate New York on the Constitution....with rancor substituting for argument."

1992.007. Bonvillian, Nancy. *Hiawatha: Founder of the Iroquois Confederacy*. New York: Chelsea House, 1992.

Page 103 quotes Benjamin Franklin's letter (1751), in which he says, in part, that "It would be a strange thing if six nations of [Indians] should be capable of forming such an union...." Drawing by John Kahionhes Fadden also used in *Exemplar of Liberty* [1991].

1992.008. Churchill, Ward. *Fantasies of the Master Race: Literature, Cinema, and the Colonization of American Indians*. Monroe, Maine: Common Courage Press, 1992.

In the chapter titled "The New Racism: A Critique of James A. Clifton's *The Invented Indian*," (pp. 163-184), reprinted from *Wicazo Sa Review* 6:2(Spring, 1991), Churchill takes up the "influence" debate through an analysis of Elisabeth Tooker's essay "The United States Constitution and the Iroquois League," first published in *Ethnohistory* [1988]. He writes (on p. 168) that Tooker attempts to "refute the 'myth' that the Six Nations Haudenosaunee Confederacy was a model of government which significantly influenced the thinking of the founding fathers in the process of conceiving the U.S. republic." Tooker, writes

Churchill, "has spent several years vociferously repeating her theme in every possible forum, and has actively attacked the credibility of scholars such as Donald Grinde and Bruce Johansen, the results of whose research have reached opposite conclusions." Churchill says that "when questioned closely on the matter at a recent academic conference, this 'expert' was forced to admit not only that she had ignored all Iroquois source material while forming her thesis, but that she was [also] quite unfamiliar with the relevant papers of John Adams, Thomas Jefferson, Benjamin Franklin, Tom Paine, and others among the U.S. founders..." Churchill cites Grinde's *The Iroquois and the Founding of the American Nation* [1977], Johansen's *Forgotten Founders* [1982, 1987], Grinde and Johansen, *Exemplar of Liberty* [1991], and Barreiro, ed., *Roots of Democracy* [1988], *et al.*

1992.009. Clark, Joe. "Excerpts From Constitutional Minister Joe Clark's Address to Canada's First Peoples Conference." *Akwesasne Notes* 23:4(Fall, 1992), pp. 17-18.

In late February, 1992, representatives of the three federalist parties in the Canadian House of Commons signed the report of the Special Joint Commission on the Renewal of Canada. The report contains a strong statement supporting Native American self-government. Clark was the chief officer of Canada's government charged with exploring new avenues of confederation when he made this speech. Minister Clark supports this case by arguing that Native Americans in North America had democratic self-government while most of Europe was still feudal. He describes the Iroquois Confederacy's emphasis on consensus. "That system was so impressive that it served as a model for Thomas Jefferson and Benjamin Franklin as they grappled with designing the American Constitution. The separation of powers, the concept of impeachment, the design of the American confederation itself -- these find their parallels in the aboriginal governments of that day." Clark reminded his audience that the word "caucus" is not Latin, but Algonquin, and that Native Americans provided not only the word, but a model for solving political problems via consensus.

1992.010. Deloria, Vine, Jr. "Comfortable Fictions and the Struggle for Turf: An Essay Review of [James Clifton's] *The Invented Indian: Cultural Fictions and Government Policies.* [New Brunswick: Transaction Publishers, 1990]. *American Indian Quarterly*, Summer, 1992, pp. 397-410.

This book of essays contains an abridged version of Tooker's 1988 *Ethnohistory* article on the U.S. Constitution and the Iroquois League. Deloria comments, on pages 402-404: "Some years ago, Bruce Johansen published a little book entitled *Forgotten Founders* [1982, 1987]....A wave of nauseous panic spread through the old-boy's network of Iroquois studies since a commoner had dared to write in a field already dominated by self-appointed experts. Donald Grinde...published *The Iroquois and the Founding of the American Nation* [1977], elaborating on this 'heresy' which was becoming an open scandal.

"Damage control measures went into effect, and soon Grinde and Johansen found their NEH grant proposals turned down by readers who emphasized the orthodox interpretation of Iroquois studies. Conservative newspaper columnists, learning of the controversy, promptly marched into historical debates of which they had no knowledge whatsoever and chastised Johansen and Grinde and proposals by the two scholars to have an open debate over the topic were generally turned aside as if mere physical contact with the two would be a sign of incipient heresy.

"Into the fray rode Elisabeth Tooker...[who] demonstrated, to her satisfaction, the impossibility of the Six Nations having any relevance at all for American constitutional thinking. Tooker's argument is so wonderfully naive and anthro-centric that it makes the informed observer of the debate weep for her inability to free herself from the blinders which adherence to anthro doctrine has required she wear."

Deloria then recapitulates Tooker's argument [See Tooker, 1988, 1990], and says that "Johansen and Grinde have collaborated now to produce *Exemplar of Liberty* [1991]...which further extends the scope of materials that must be considered to make any sense out of this issue."

Recalling a meeting of the American Anthropological Association at which he and Tooker debated this issue, Deloria writes that after he asserted that John Locke's attempt to set up a landed aristocracy in North Carolina discredited him in the eyes of the colonists, "Tooker bolted into the aisle, shrieking, 'Tell that to your friends! Tell that to your friends!'"

Deloria concludes: "This debate has not really been joined properly because what Johansen and Grinde are saying is simply that considerably more material must be examined before hard and fast conclusions are drawn. Tooker's argument, it seems to me, is simply that materials, and arrangement of these materials which the entrenched scholars of anthropology have amassed, are sufficient to answer all questions regarding the Six Nations -- period. The real debate, therefore, is over authority: to whom shall we listen -- about anything? Here the credentials of the past, no matter how valiantly won, are just not enough to dominate or close debate on a subject -- period." This critique was developed from observation of the debate, and publications provided by some of its advocates.

1992.011. Jacobs, Wilbur. "The American Indian Legacy of Freedom and Liberty." *American Indian Culture & Research Journal* 16:4(1992), pp. 185-193.

In this commentary regarding the debate over the "influence" issue, Jacobs, professor emeritus at the University of California -- Santa Barbara, examines *Exemplar of Liberty* [Grinde and Johansen, 1991] in light of his readings in history while a research scholar at the Huntington Library. "Grinde and Johansen are doing pioneering work in Indian history, correcting the misdirected thinking of certain colonial historians and anthropologists. In so doing, they are spreading a new light of understanding and setting forth new themes for general American history and government." Jacobs examines the writings on the subject by Temple University anthropology professor Elisabeth Tooker, and finds support for Johansen and Grinde's construction of history in the works of Lawrence H. Gipson, who observed that European colonists were exposed to Native American diplomacy and forms of governance on a repeated basis from the earliest years of settlement, setting a precedent for Benjamin Franklin's use of an Iroquois confederate model in his Albany Plan of Union and Articles of Confederation. Jacobs also calls on his readings of Carl L. Becker and William Brandon.

1992.012. Jaimes, M. Annette. *The State of Native America: Genocide, Colonization, and Resistance.* Boston: South End Press, 1992.

Chapter 3 ("Self-Determination and Subordination: The Past, Present, and Future of American Indian Self-Governance," by Rebecca L. Robbins) begins with a brief description of the Iroquois Confederacy. Robbins observes that pre-contact political systems in the Americas were sophisticated and complex. She adds: (on page 87): "Certain of the structures and principles of indigenous governance, notably those drawn from the Haudenosaunee (Iroquois) Confederacy...were so advanced that they were consciously utilized as a primary model upon which the U.S. Constitution was formulated and the federal government created." Robbins cites Grinde and Johansen's early books [1977, 1982, 1987], as well as *Exemplar of Liberty* [1991], Burton [1988], and Barreiro, *Roots of Democracy* [1988].

1992.013. James, Jewell Praying Wolf, in Kurt Russo, ed., *Our People, Our Land*. Bellingham, Washington: Lummi Tribe and Kluckhohn Center, 1992, pp. 32-35.

Page 33: "It is with irony [that] we note that the U.S. Congress has finally recognized that the American Indian confederacies and societies were a great influence in the the formation of America's form of constitutional democracy," said James, a lineal descendent of Chief Seal'th, in remarks prepared for a conference sponsored by the Lummis, *et al.* in Seattle, during October of 1991. James lists a number of native contributions, such as the caucus system to reach consensus, the custom of giving the respect of silence to speakers (so unlike the British Parliament), checks and balances, and individual rights. "the next irony," says James, is "the motivating influence [that] Indian concepts of communalism had upon the evolution of Communism...and the duty of society to care for the old, the weak, and the war-injured." The "irony" to which James refers is that the United States has used its Constitution to justify the taking of native land and resources, while Communism also oppressed native peoples in the former Soviet Union.

1992.014. Johansen, Bruce E. "Remembering the Forgotten Founders." in Kurt Russo, ed., *Our People, Our Land: Perspectives on the Columbus Quincentenary*. Bellingham, WA: Lummi Tribe and Kluckhohn Center, 1992.

Printed proceedings of a conference held in Seattle during October, 1991. "Remembering the Forgotten Founders" is the written text of a presentation by Johansen at that conference. Phil Lucas, Choctaw filmmaker who had known Johansen since the late 1970s, when both worked in Seattle, suggested the theme to organizers of this conference, which was held as a counterpoint to Columbus Day.

1992.015. Johansen. "Commentary." *Akwe:kon Journal* 9:4(Winter, 1992), p. 3.

This is a reply to William Starna's allegations that assertions of Haudenosaunee (Iroquois) influence on the development of democracy are "nonsense." Editing and timely publication of the New York State Education Department curriculum guide *Haudenosaunee: Past, Present Future* is advised. Starna had advised scrapping the guide in protest of references to the Iroquois and democracy.

1992.016. Landsman, Gail H. "The 'Other' as Political Symbol: Images of the Indians in the Woman Suffrage Movement," *Ethnohistory* 39:1(Summer, 1992), pp. 247-284.

Using primary sources also used by Sally Roesch Wagner, Landsman describes the ways in which Native American (particularly Iroquois) examples helped shape the ideology of the women's movement from 1848 to 1920. Landsman then plugs the documentary record into an ethnohistorical framework, arguing that while the early suffragists utilized the Indian image extensively, they were activists who formed their opinions "not through the discovery of objective truth but in the context of validating and/or advancing the story of woman suffrage." (p. 252) This article indicates the important role that mythmaking has played in the shaping of ideological movements throughout history. Landsman mentions the overall "influence " debate (citing Grinde, Johansen, and Tooker), but says only that such ideas "are...open to scholarly debate and ethnohistorical research." (p. 252) [Files contain a letter from Landsman, dated Feb. 25, 1993, which assert her independence of work by Sally Wagner, as well as differences between her arguments and those of Starna, and other anthropologists].

1992.017. Landsman, Gail. H., and Sara Ciborski. "Representation and Politics: Contested Histories of the Iroquois." *Cultural Anthropology* 7(4) November, 1992, pp. 425-447.

This analysis of the controversy surrounding the New York State Department of Education curriculum guide *Haudenosaunee: Past, Present, Future* delves into "the politics of historical representation and the social construction of knowledge," [p. 425], asserting that Iroquois traditionalists and scholars who support their case for "influence" have adopted the tactics and standards of "objectivist history" (i.e. documentary research) to support the case. The essay then contradicts itself by calling the Iroquois' scholarly tactics "radical traditionalist ethnicity" [p. 441]. This confusion is compounded by an abundance of unattributed quotations from "mainstream Iroquoianists," who have criticized the guide and the "influence thesis" in general. Page after page asserting that "one scholar" at "a conference" said this or that gives the paper an air of small-town gossip rather than scholarship. Landsman and Ciborski also suffer from a problem that seems endemic among "mainstream Iroquois experts:" the temptation to package other scholars' (as well as Iroquois) motives to fit predetermined academic categories, as in their discussion of who is, and isn't, practicing "objectivist" history.

1992.018. Lewis, Martin W. *Green Delusions: An Environmentalist Critique of Radical Environmentalism.* Durham, N. C.: Duke University Press, 1992.

On page 92 of *Green Delusions*, Lewis, an assistant professor of geography at George Washington University, argues that participatory democracy may not eliminate social repression. Instead, he believes it perpetuates "a tyranny of long-winded individuals [who are] immune to boredom." Lewis believes that the inefficiency of participatory democracy uses more of the earth's resources for decision making than other forms of government. "Unable to hold up their own or their forebears' experimental efforts in communal living," writes Lewis, "They [eco-radicals] have turned instead to indigenous American social organization. One popular model of participatory democracy is the Iroquois Confederacy..." Lewis finds the Iroquois to be "a particularly ill-considered exemplar. Admiring the Iroquois political system of that era for its democracy is akin to praising Nazi Germany for its enlightened forestry. The Five Nations not only engaged in a highly successful campaign of ethnocide against their competitors in the fur trade, the Hurons, but they also raised the torture of war captives (those whom they chose not to adopt, at any rate) to a high art."

1992.019. Limbaugh, Rush. *The Way Things Ought to Be.* New York: Pocket Books, 1992.

Page 204: "Multiculturalism is billed as a way to make Americans more sensitive to the diverse cultural backgrounds of people in this country. It's time we blew the whistle on that. What is being taught under the guise of multiculturalism is worse than historical revisionism. It's more than a distortion of facts. It's the elimination of facts. In some schools, kids are being taught that the ideas of the Constitution were borrowed from the Iroquois Indians and that Africans discovered America."

1992.020. Lyons, Oren, John Mohawk, Vine Deloria, Jr., Laurence Hauptman, Howard Berman, Donald Grinde, Jr., Curtis Berkey and Robert Venables. *Exiled in the Land of the Free: Democracy, Indian Nations, and the U.S. Constitution.* Santa Fe, N.M.: Clear Light Publishers, 1992.

Wide-ranging discussion of native democratic traditions, and how recognition of their precedence could shape present-day law affecting American Indians. This collection of essays is the perfect antidote to Clifton's *Invented Indian* [1990, reviewed by Deloria 1992, above]. The idea that Native American confederacies, principally the Iroquois, contributed to the evolution of democracy is mentioned in the book's preface, by Senator Daniel Inouye, and in its foreword, by Peter Matthiessen. The theme is raised again at the beginning of the Introduction, by Lyons and Mohawk, and developed extensively in essays by Venables ("American Indian Influences on the America of the Founding Fathers"), and Grinde ("Iroquois Political Theory and the Roots of American Democracy"). The debate over the idea is discussed in Mohawk's essay "Indians and Democracy: No One Ever Told Us."

1992.021. Maybury-Lewis, David. *Millennium: Tribal Wisdom and the Modern World.* New York: Viking, 1992.

This survey of aboriginal cultures around the world, prepared by Cultural Survival of Cambridge, Mass., contains a well-developed description of the Iroquois League's origins and operations. It also mentions Cannassatego's advice to the colonies on unification in 1744, and Benjamin Franklin's use of the theme in the early 1750s. Both Franklin and Jefferson were impressed by Indians' political systems, especially regarding egalitarianism. "There is an argument raging currently over whether or not the founding fathers of the United States of America consciously modelled their new nation on the Iroquois Confederacy. It seems to me, however, that the important thing is not whether they did or did not, but the fact that they *could* have. There were, after all, no models in Europe at that time for the kind of federal republic that the Americans established." Maybury-Lewis cites *Forgotten Founders*.

1992.022. Oshinsky, David M. [Review: Schlesinger, *Disuniting of America*] *The New Leader*, March 9, 1992, p. 19.

Again, a reviewer trumpets Schlesinger's errors of fact regarding the New York State "Curriculum of Inclusion" guide Haudenosaunee: *Past, Present, Future*. Again, we expect to see New York high school students learning that the Iroquois Confederacy was an important foundation for the U.S. Constitution. This is supposed to be part of "an all-out assault on our national core," and an indication that "assimilation was out; victimization was in." Somehow, the facts of the matter get lost in a collusional party of fabrication by author and reviewer.

1992.023. Royal, Robert. *1492 and All That.* Washington, D.C.: Ethics and Public Policy Center, 1992.

This brief book raises the "influence" issue on pp. 152 and 153: "The Iroquois had perhaps the most highly developed Native American political association in North America....In 1987, the U.S. Congress formally proclaimed that the Iroquois played an important role in the creation of American democracy. As a result, American schoolchildren are taught today that the Iroquois Confederation was a model for the American Founders as they began to consider how to organize the thirteen independent former colonies...." Royal maintains that "a few...passages" in historical records indicate this, and he quotes from Benjamin Franklin's 1751 letter to his printing partner James Parker to this effect. However, Royal believes that no one investigated the structure of the Confederacy until the 1840s, a reference to Lewis Henry Morgan, who is not named in his text. Consequently, he writes, the Iroquois role "in shaping the Constitution in any serious way is doubtful to say the least." Judging from his references, Royal seems unaware that any scholarly work has been done supporting the idea. He cites Tooker [1988], calling her essay refuting the "influence thesis" "a valuable review of the claims and counterclaims." Royal also cites Clifton's *Invented Indian* [1990, reviewed by Deloria, 1992], and Schlesinger, *Disuniting of America* [1992].

1992.024. Schlesinger, Arthur M., Jr. *The Disuniting of America.* New York: W.W. Norton, 1992.

Schlesinger (on pages 96-98) takes issue with "history-for self-esteem," or "feel-good history," by which, he says, self-interested minority groups seek to express their points of view in school curricula. His target here is the New York State "Curriculum of Inclusion," which includes a Native American study guide entitled *Haudenosaunee* [Iroquois]: *Past, Present, Future*. This curriculum guide had been the object of a bureaucratic ideological battle within the State Department of Education for at least five years by 1992. Scholars on both sides of the issue have worked as consultants to this study under contract with the New York State Education Department. Until 1992, the guide contained references to the "influence thesis," which were reportedly excised after complaints by people to whom Vine Deloria, Jr. referred in his essay [1992] as "the old-boys' network of anthropology." Page 97: "In New York the curriculum for 11th-grade history tells students that there were three 'foundations' for the Constitution: the European Enlightenment, the 'Haudenosaunee political system,' and the antecedent colonial experience....How many experts on the American Constitution would endorse this stirring tribute to the 'Haudenosaunee political system'? How many have heard of that system? Whatever influence the Iroquois confederacy had on the framers of the Constitution was marginal; on European intellectuals, it was marginal to the point of invisibility. No other state curriculum offers this analysis of the making of the Constitution. But then no other state has so effective an Iroquois lobby."

Schlesinger's book contains no footnotes or endnotes, so it is unknown what works he consulted before composing the above statements. He read *Forgotten Founders* in 1982 and endorsed it: "*Forgotten Founders* is a tour-de-force of ingenious and elegant scholarship offering justice at last to the Indian contributions to the American Constitution." [Letter, Schlesinger to Lovell Thompson, publisher, Gambit, Inc., 1982].

1992.025. Stannard, David E. *American Holocaust: Columbus and the Conquest of the New World.* New York: Oxford University Press, 1992.

Pages 28-30: "Probably the most common association that is made with the congregations of northeastern cultures concerns their sophisticated domestic political systems....such as the Five Nation Confederacy of the Iroquois....Many writers, both historians and anthropologists, have argued that the League was a model for the United States Constitution, although much controversy continues to surround that assertion. The debate focuses largely on the *extent* of Iroquois influence on Euro-American political thought, however, since no one denies that there was some influence." Other writers have discussed the impact of the new United States on Europe, writes Stannard. "In any case, however the controversy over Iroquois influence is decided, it will not minimize the Iroquois achievement..." [emphasis in original]. Stannard cites the Tooker-Johansen exchange in *Ethnohistory* [1988, 1990] and Johansen and Grinde, "Precedents," in *American Indian Culture & Research Journal* [1990]. This powerful book builds a case that the ethnocide practiced against native peoples in the Americas during the previous 500 years comprises the greatest holocaust in human history. Stannard is a historian of demography with a specialty in holocausts.

1992.026. Tack, Alan, [Review of *Exemplar of Liberty* (1991)], in *Native Peoples* [Phoenix], Summer, 1992, p. 72.

"Clearly, the pervasive and persistent influence of American Indian political systems on modern democracy and the American character lend this book its life and power. The authors' hope is that some day we may all 'join hands and celebrate the diverse roots of the American democratic tradition without the blinders of indifference and cultural arrogance.' This book nurtures that hope by helping us understand American democracy as a unique synthesis of Native American and European ideas..."

1992.027. Trosper, Ronald L. "Mind Sets and Economic Development on Indian Reservations," in Stephen Cornell and Joseph P. Kalt, eds., *What Can Tribes Do? Strategies and Institutions in American Indian Economic Development*. Los Angeles: UCLA American Indian Studies Center, 1992.

On page 327, Trosper is discussing Native American methods of building political consensus in systems with checks and balances. "The Iroquois, of course, are famous," he writes, footnoting Johansen and Grinde, "A Recent Historiography" [1990].

1992.028. Wagner, Sally Roesch. "The Iroquois Influence on Women's Rights." *Akwe:kon Journal* (formerly *Northeast Indian Quarterly*) 9:1(Spring, 1992), pp. 4-15.

This is Sally Roesch Wagner's most detailed published description to date of how contact with Iroquois people helped shape the thoughts of Elizabeth Cady Stanton, Matilda Joslyn Gage, and other founders of modern American feminism. See also: Wagner [1988, 1989] and Grinde and Johansen, *Exemplar of Liberty* [1991] Chapter 11 ("Persistence of an Idea") [1991].

1992.029. Wolfson, Evelyn. *The Iroquois: People of the Northeast.* Brookfield, CT: Millbrook Press, 1992.

This children's book opens its first chapter (on page 9) by asking: "Did you know that America's founding fathers were inspired by the Iroquois in their search for a form of government for America's colonies?" The book outlines Iroquois culture, including their political system. Cannassatego's advice in 1744 that the colonists form a union like that of the Iroquois (p. 43). On p. 56, Wolfson notes the similarity of Franklin's Albany Plan of 1754 and the Iroquois Great Law of Peace. The book references Grinde [1977], Johansen [1982, 1987] and Grinde and Johansen [1991].

1992.030. Wright, Ronald. *Stolen Continents: The Americas Through Indian Eyes Since 1492.* Boston: Houghton-Mifflin, 1992.

Pages 115-116: The Iroquois Confederacy "still survive[s], still fighting for recognition of a nationhood that they believe they never surrendered to the parvenus who built the United States and Canada around them. They also feel ironic pride that European colonists took the Iroquois Confederacy as a model when contemplating a union of their own." Wright then recounts some of the events in this chain of circumstances, such as the speech by Onondaga sachem Cannassatego at Lancaster in 1744 calling on the colonists to emulate the confederacy. Wright places Benjamin Franklin at that meeting, a factual error. Franklin, still a printer by trade in 1744, published the proceedings of the Lancaster Treaty Conference, so he was undoubtedly familiar with Cannassatego's words. He did not attend treaty councils personally until the 1750s, however. Wright correctly points out that the bundle of arrows on the U.S. Great Seal is an Iroquois symbol, and that originally the bundle was to have contained five arrows (for the five original Iroquois nations) rather than 13, one for each original state. Wright describes the operation of the Iroquois League and historic comment on it through page 120. He returns to the subject on pp. 320-342, ending with the 1990 confrontation at Oka, Quebec. Wright cites early books by Grinde and Johansen [1977, 1982, 1987], as well as Tooker's article [1988], and Johansen's reply in *Ethnohistory* [1988, 1990].

Popular Magazines and Newspapers

1992.031. _____. "The Archaeologists Discover the Last of the Philistines." Washington *Times*, October 3, 1992, p. B-2.

This editorial ridicules recent archaeological work indicating that the Philistines, whom the editorial calls "boors, uncultured wretches and barbarians" actually may have been Greeks possessed of a high culture. The editorial opens: "Historical revisionism seems to be getting entirely out of hand. First, we heard that Columbus wasn't the Renaissance man we were told he was. Then, 'multiculturalists' claimed that the Iroquois Indians influenced the Founding Fathers. Now...we learn that archaeologists are reconsidering the character of the Philistines...." This is one of many examples of *reductio ad absurdum* argument against the "influence" idea.

1992.032. _____. "Manhattan Neighborhoods." *Newsday*, January 13, 1992, p. 21.

"People Against Sexual Abuse has developed and produced...a workshop for formerly undocumented aliens applying for citizenship that explains the Bill of Rights. The program, called Roots of Democracy...stresses the relationship of the U.S. Constitution to the Iroquois Indians' Great Law of Peace."

1992.033. Associated Press, in Syracuse *Post-Standard*, January 12, 1992.

At a gathering on the Seminole reservation, Florida, James Jumper said: "the Constitution is based on the Iroquois Nation's philosophy."

1992.034. Beaton, Danny, and Lindsey Mitchell. "We Are the People Columbus Discovered." Toronto *Star*, January 3, 1992, p. A-17.

Before the arrival of Columbus, the two authors write in this opinion column, native nations in the Americas had sophisticated political systems which solved problems through consensus and were strongly influenced by women.

1992.035. Bosveld, Jane. "Forgotten Founders: Did the Great Law of Peace, the Constitution of the Iroquois Nation, Help Shape Democracy and Federalism?" *Omni*, Feb., 1992, p. 33.

Bosveld surveys the debate, then concludes, borrowing from Jack Weatherford, that "the Indian model of democracy was replaced [after 1800] by the Greek model, in which slavery was permitted. It was a shift in thinking that rationalized the fate of African-Americans and laid the foundation for displacement and genocide of Native Americans. Perhaps it is time to include the Great Law of Peace in American textbooks." As its title indicates, this piece is based in part on *Forgotten Founders* [1982, 1987].

1992.036. Brookhiser, Richard. [Review of Schlesinger, *Disuniting America*] *National Review*, May 11, 1992, p. 49.

With Schlesinger, Brookhiser takes aim at purveyors of multiculturalism, "...'Scholars' who claim that the Constitution was cribbed from the Iroquois, or that ancient Egypt was a black civilization whose wisdom was plundered by Alexander the Great and slipped to his tutor Aristotle."

1992.037. Buchanan, Patrick J. "America's Cultural War." Atlanta *Constitution*, September 15, 1992, p. A-15.

"The cultural war is already raging in our public schools. In history texts, Benedict Arnold's treason at West Point has been dropped. So has the story of Nathan Hale, the boy patriot who spied on the British and went to the gallows with the defiant cry, 'I regret that I have but one life to give for my country.' Elsewhere, they teach that our Constitution was plagiarized from the Iroquois, and that Western science was stolen from sub-Sahara Africa." *Whew!*

1992.038. Dahl, Katherine. [Review, Lyons, *et al.*, *Exiled in the Land of the Free*(1992)]. *Library Journal*, vol. 117, No. 19 (November 15, 1992), p. 88.

"That the founding fathers were philosophically and culturally influenced by the Indian nations is explained...to any doubter's or disbeliever's satisfaction" by *Exiled*, says Dahl. "Truly a great book," she says of *Exiled*, which is "an effective antidote for the Columbus...hoopla."

1992.039. Diakiw, Jerry. "Our Culture's Native Roots." Toronto *Star*, July 21, 1992, p. A-19.

In an opinion piece, Diakiw surveys general Canadian culture's debt to native precedents, including Montaigne's use of information supplied him by visitors to the Iroquois. He also quotes Frederich Engels' surprise at reading Lewis Henry Morgan's accounts of Iroquois society with its lack of class structure. He asserts that Karl Marx's sense of feminism was shaped by studying Morgan on the matrilineal nature of Iroquois society. Of the Iroquois Confederacy, Diakiw says "it had a profound influence on both the American and Canadian systems of government." He details the remarks on colonial union by Cannassatego at the 1744 Lancaster Treaty Council, and Benjamin Franklin's use of it, asserting that the three-tier system of federalism used in the United States and Canada is an inheritance of Iroquois inspiration. Canada, in particular, merged this system with the English parliamentary tradition, he says. This piece was one of several that used Iroquois examples in debates over a new Canadian constitution during the early 1990s.

1992.040. Doxtater, Mike. "The Constitution of the Five Nations." *The Indigenous Voices* (Hamilton, Ontario, Canada), August/September, 1992, pp. 1, 3.

This article in a Native American newspaper outlines the political structure and procedures of the Iroquois Confederacy, and briefly traces its influence on Benjamin Franklin, the German philosopher Hegel, as well as Marx and Engels. The article also notes that Marxian philosophy contains elements contrary to the philosophy of the Great Law of Peace. The article cites Weatherford, *Indian Givers* [1988].

1992.041. Evans-Pritchard, Ambrose. "Down with DWEMs -- America's New Apartheid." *The Daily Telegraph* [London], August 30, 1992, Books, p. 15.

In this review of Arthur Schlesinger, Jr.'s book *Disuniting of America*, Evans-Pritchard comes out in defense of DWEMs -- Dead, White, European Males -- whom he says are suffering at the hands of "the American race-relations industry, [which is] amply subsidized by the public purse." "Education in America is becoming a form of therapy," he writes, with examples: "Black school children in Portland, Oregon, are taught that Africans discovered America. In New York, the curriculum guide for 11th-grade history tells students that the Haudenosaunee political system of the Iroquois Indians was the inspiration for the American constitution..." As has been pointed out elsewhere, the proposed curriculum over which Schlesinger and this writer are knashing their teeth was drafted, but not implemented by the state.

1992.042. Galbraith, Jane. "Costner to Bring Indian History to CBS in 1994..." Los Angeles *Times*, July 30, 1992, p. F-1 [Entertainment].

This is a background report on plans being made by Kevin Costner and associates, with $8 million of Coster's money, to produce a documentary series on American Indians to be broadcast on CBS. The producers are quoted as saying that "Democracy has roots in the Iroquois."

1992.043. Harjo, Suzan Shown. "Columbus: Discoverer or Despoiler? American Indians Still Reeling from Genocide." Dallas *Morning News*, October 11, 1992, p. 1-J.

In this 3,000-word survey of the five centuries since Columbus' first landfall in the Americas, Suzan Shown Harjo characterizes Columbus Day as "a holiday that represents native national, cultural, and family genocide." The myth of "discovery" often comes with a myth about democracy, despite the lack of practicing democratic models in Europe. "It was here, in the Iroquois...and other confederacies, where Benjamin Franklin, Thomas Jefferson, and other Founding Fathers found longstanding working models of Native nations united for peacetime purposes....The basic precept of democracy -- inherent sovereignty of the individual -- was found here." Ironically, she says, today the system to which Indians so vitally contributed refuses to recognize many native religious rights.

1992.044. Harris, John F. "Arthur Schlesinger's Education in Controversy..." [Review of Schlesinger, *Disuniting America*] Washington *Post*, June 1, 1992, p. B-1.

Another dump on the New York State Education curriculum *Haudenosaunee: Past, Present, Future* by an uncomprehending critic. "The state's official curriculum, for example, tells students that the thinking of the Iroquois Confederacy was an important influence on the framers of the U.S. Constitution." No one seems to have watched the history of this guide besides the Iroquois themselves, who watched it rot in the state's education bureaucracy after unfavorable reviews from various Iroquois "experts."

1992.045. Hume, Stephen. "Bigotry Wrapped in Nationalist Banner." Vancouver *Sun*, February 21, 1992, p. A-13.

Hume is addressing the question of Quebec's claim for "special status" in a newly defined Canadian confederation. He says that advocates of Quebec's sovereignty are being hypocritical when they refuse to allow sovereignty for First Peoples inside the province's borders. Orvide Mercredi is said to have recently made this argument, for which he was criticized by several Quebec politicians. "Consider the monumental insult Mercredi must feel in downtown Montreal where the first encounter between the founders [of Quebec] and the Iroquois is celebrated with a disgusting depiction of Paul de Chomeday blowing out a chief's brains with his pistol....The Indian he killed already had a constitution so sophisticated that the United States borrowed it...."

1992.046. Jensen, Erik M. "Iroquois Didn't Write U.S. Constitution." *Cleveland Plain Dealer*, August 1, 1992.

Jensen, professor of Law at Case Western University, refutes assertions of influence along lines similar to his refutation of Greg Schaaf in *The American Indian Law Review* 15:2(1991), described below. Jensen names none of the scholars that he says are spreading this "bogus history," and the newspaper format allows no references, so it's tough to tell at whom Professor Jensen is aiming this barrage of buzzwords.

1992.047. Johnson, Gordon K. "Constitution is Inspired." [Letter to the editor] Calgary *Herald*, October 18, 1992, p. A-7.

Writing in the context of Canada's constitutional debate, Johnson says "There have been two streams of democracy," one from the European

Enlightenment, the other from our tribal heritage, "which [has] been successful [in] ancient Greece, the Swiss cantons, and the Iroquois Confederacy." Canada faces the problem of how to accommodate diverse nationalities and other groups in a common territory, says Johnson. "We have no Thomas Jefferson, but we do have Orvide Mercredi and the Inuit mothers and grandmothers of confederation." This is one of several citations of Iroquois precedent during debates over a new constitution for Canada in the early 1990s.

1992.048. Kaye, Mary. "The Road to Beauty." *Sassy*, October, 1992, pp. 76-78, 90-91.

Tucked among articles with titles such as "Axl Rose: Clothes Horse," and "Beauty Tips for Procrastinators," Kaye contributes an article headed (on the magazine's cover) "Why Our Screwed-up Planet Needs Native Americans." While most of the article relates the author's personal experiences among the Navajo, on page 78, she writes: "These days the brainwashing is more insidious...textbooks virtually ignore Native American contributions (did you know, for example, that parts of Iroquois law were incorporated into the American Constitution?)...."

1992.049. Kermode, Frank. "Whose History is Bunk." New York *Times*, February 23, 1992, Section 7, Page 3 [Book Review].

Kermode is reviewing several recent books on "political correctness," two of which [Schlesinger, *Disuniting of America* and Berman, *Debating P.C.*] take up the "influence" issue. Reviewing Schlesinger's book, Kermode paraphrases his argument but does not comment on it: "Honest history cannot regard the European origins of culture and Constitution as poisonous." [One wonders: *who* is regarding them as poisonous?] In the book edited by Berman, Diane Ravitch contributes an essay that opposes the "influence" idea. Kermode comments: "...Ms. Ravitch is wrong to deny the influence of the Iroquois (Haudenosaunee) on Upstate New York on the Constitution....with rancor substituting for argument."

1992.050. Knox, Bernard. "The Oldest Dead White European Males: Ancient Greece." *The New Republic* 206:21 (May 25, 1992), p. 27.

This is a survey of the debts that modern society owes to the Greeks, which also develops debates over male dominance and slavery in ancient Greek society. Near the end of his article, Knox appends this disclaimer: "All this does not entitle us, of course, to discard the results of the re-evaluation of Greek culture that has emphasized its 'otherness,' the attitudes and institutions that resemble those of Egypt and Babylon, not to mention those of Lafitau's Algonquins, Hurons, and Iroquois."

1992.051. Lunner, Chet. "A Primer On the First People." [Gannett News Service] October 12, 1992.

Released on the 500th anniversary of Columbus' first landfall in the Americas, this newswire piece contains a lengthy, detailed account of the circumstances which compelled Benjamin Franklin and other colonial leaders to meet Iroquois sachems and adopt some of their political practices as the English colonies sought a model on which to unite. Lunner begins with Cannassatego's advice that the British colonists unify in 1744, and Franklin's use of similar concepts in the Albany Plan of Union and Articles of Confederation. Lunner quotes from an interview with Jack Weatherford and cites his 1988 title *Indian Givers*.

1992.052. Mander, Jerry. "Wisdom from Other Cultures." [Review of Maybury-Lewis, *Millennium*, 1992] San Francisco *Chronicle*, April 26, 1992, Sunday Review, p. 3.

According to Mander, author of *In the Absence of the Sacred* [1991], *Millennium* is "an immensely valuable collection of rare information about dozens of the world's still-viable native societies." The book "takes us through native medical practice and pharmacology, religious philosophy, and numerous examples of democratic forms of governance, notably the Iroquois,' whose Great Law was surely the main model for the U.S. Constitution."

1992.053. Mander, Jerry. [Review of Nabokov, *Native American Testimony*] *The Nation*, April 6, 1992, p. 461.

Mander observes that during the recent bicentennial of the U.S. Constitution, "not one word appeared in the official proceedings and damned few in the press about the critical role that Indian political thinkers and the Iroquois Confederacy Great Law (created centuries before Columbus' arrival) had in influencing the concepts of governance then being developed by our 'Founding Fathers.'" [Johansen talked with Warren Burger, head of the bicentennial commission, during a conference at the University of South Dakota, Vermillion, during October, 1988. He was interested enough to stay up late the same night reading a copy of *Forgotten Founders* I gave him. We were both staying at the Super 8 Motel. As I checked out, he came down the hall and asked me to stop -- he wanted to tell me how much he appreciated the new knowledge. He referred me to staff, who ignored the idea.]

1992.054. McGhee, Robert. "Time to Put the Facts Ahead of the Myths About Columbus." Ottawa *Citizen*, October 14, 1992, p. A-11.

In an op-ed column, McGhee is replying to Michael Berliner of the Ayn Rand Institute, who described Columbus as having brought "undreamed-of benefits" to the aboriginal peoples of the Americas. In his refutation of Berliner's arguments, McGhee says that "modern Western civilization is not a product developed solely by Europeans, as assumed by Berliner." McGhee cites a number of food crops first used by native peoples of the Americas. He adds: "The American constitution and its concept of democracy may owe much, it has been suggested, to the political concepts of the Iroquois and other Native American peoples." McGhee is an archaeologist with the Canadian Museum of Civilization.

1992.055. Menard, Louis. "School Daze: Multicultural Education." *Harper's Bazaar*, September, 1992, p. 380.

This 2,400-word discussion of the debate over multicultural education stakes out New York State as a major battle front, because of the "Curriculum of Inclusion," including its "recommendation that pupils be taught about the influence of the Haudenosaunee political system (of the Iroquois tribes in Upstate New York, in case you've forgotten) on the U.S. Constitution." The snippish tone of the piece reveals Menard's near-total ignorance of early American history, at least as regards the Iroquois and their political system.

1992.056. Mitchell, Peter. "A Conversation With Buchanan." Orlando *Sentinel*, February 27, 1992, p. A-5.

What is a professor to do when he finds the subject of his Ph.D. dissertation used as campaign fodder by a stump-preaching politician? Patrick Buchanan is quoted here as saying: "When you see the idiocy that somehow the American Constitution is a direct descendant of the Iroquois Confederation documents -- this is all trash and nonsense. The effort is to turn future Americans into people who despise their own history and background...."

1992.057. Nells, Karen. "PEF Officials Confront Cuomo at State Museum," Albany *Times Union*, October 6, 1992, pp. B-1, B-6.

New York State public employees confronted Governor Cuomo as he opened an exhibit on Iroquois life at the New York State Museum in Albany. In his speech opening the exhibit, Cuomo "credited the Iroquois people with developing the democratic principles that form the basis of the U. S. Constitution....'The evidence is strong that the Founding Fathers were greatly influenced by the framework of the Iroquois Nation.'" William Starna, chair of anthropology at the State University of New York at Oneonta, is quoted as saying that is "one of the damnedest, silliest ideas I've ever heard....The literature has absolutely devastated the argument that the Iroquois Constitution influenced the U.S. Constitution."

1992.058. O'Donnell, J. H., III. [Review of *Exemplar of Liberty*(1991)]. *CHOICE*, July/August 1992, p. 1745.

O'Donnell outlines the contents of *Exemplar of Liberty*, but does not really review the book. He restates the authors' "admission" (his word) that the ideas in the book are "controversial," and recommends it for research libraries "where readers will find available the sources appropriate for comparison and analysis."

1992.59. *Rethinking Schools*, special issue, *Rethinking Columbus*, n.d.

Page 44 describes Iroquois influence on shaping of the Constitution, citing *Forgotten Founders*.

1992.060. Shah, Reena. "When the Melting Pot Breaks Down." [Review of Schlesinger, *Disuniting of America*] St. Petersburg [Florida] *Times*, April 5, 1992, p. 4-D.

Yet another reviewer bites on Schlesinger's assertion that high-school juniors in New York State are being force-fed fantasies of Iroquois political prowess. Such mileage out of a couple of unintentionally fictional sentences! "Why is it obligatory to insist that the Iroquois inspired the U.S. Constitution, but irrelevant to consider that W.E.B. Dubois admiringly devoured Pitt, Sheridan, Shakespeare, and Balzac?"

1992.061. Smith, Robert L. "Democracy, Indian Style." Syracuse *Post-Standard*, Dec. 28, 1992, pp. B-1, B-5.

This review of Oren Lyons, *et al.*, *Exiled in the Land of the Free* [1992] quotes Lyons' contention that the United States adopted only parts of Iroquois and other native democratic systems. The founders compromised with their European heritage by permitting slavery [in the southern states] and ignoring the rights of women, as well as making the vote initially contingent on property ownership. Reviewer Smith notes that most of the book's co-authors subscribe to the "influence school." "...[T]he authors point to Iroquois concepts, such as federalism, untested in Europe, that found their way into the Constitution." Benjamin Franklin's role is noted. Smith ignores the fact that some examples of confederation *do* exist in European history, although they were not practiced (as were Native American confederacies) within eyeshot of the United States' founders. European confederacies were analyzed in John Adams' *Defence of the Constitutions...*, along with the Iroquois system.

1992.062. Steele, Mike. "Heart of the Beast Offers Witty, Instructive Version of History of America." Minneapolis *Star-Tribune*, February 3, 1992, p. 5-E.

Steele reviews "Discover America," In the Heart of the Beast Puppet and Mask Theatre's "alternative look at pre-and-post-Columbus America." He calls it "devilishly witty and seductively charming." This is a children's show that develops American history from a non-European point of view. The show takes its audience through history, and shows that Native American civilizations "are anything but savage and often quite creative and complex -- the Iroquois experimented with democracy long before royal Europe thought of it."

1992.063. Stoute, Lenny. "Buffy's Back With First Album in 15 Years." Toronto *Star*, March 17, 1992, p. C-4.

The singer Buffy Sainte-Marie is interviewed on the road in Toronto. She is quoted as saying that "Right now, people all over the world are dissatisfied and looking for new ways of government. They could learn, for instance, from the Iroquois Confederacy, from which the American Constitution derives." Sainte-Marie says that the Constitution "didn't go far enough. The Europeans couldn't handle the female roles in the Iroquois system and choose to ignore them. From there, it's a short jump to ignoring the rights of females altogether."

1992.064. Switzer, Norah L. "Parliamentary Democracy." [Letter to the editor] Los Angeles *Times*, August 25, 1992, p. B-6.

Switzer takes issue with an editorial in the *Times* suggesting that the United States consider a parliamentary system. The writer uses Jack Weatherford's assertion in *Indian Givers* [1988] that "our nation's legislation [legislative system] was founded directly on the principles of the Iroquois League of Nations in which the 'purpose of debate...was to persuade and educate, not to confront...'" Switzer contends that the two major parties that evolved after the Constitution was ratified have effectively imposed a *de facto* parliamentary system, and that "our legislators would be wise to follow the example set by the Iroquois speakers, one good enough to impress the Founding Fathers into modelling our legislative system after it.

1992.065. Tallman, Valerie. "Tribal Nations Air Concerns Before the United Nations." *Indian Country Today*, December 24, 1992.

Tallman reports on a speech by Oren Lyons at the United Nations, part of proceedings to begin the 1993 Year of Indigenous Peoples. As part of her report on Lyons speech, Tallman notes that Lyons "is author of a new book, *Exiled in the Land of the Free*, which documents the Native origins of democracy and illustrates the link between the Iroquois Confederacy's Great Law of Peace and the U. S. Constitution."

1992.066. Tamblyn, Ian. "Country's Economic Ills Cited as Reason for Rejection of Deal." Calgary *Herald*, October 29, 1992, p. A-5.

This article surveys reactions to the defeat of the Charlottetown Accord in Canada. One of the people responding is Ruth Norton, education officer with the Assembly of First Nations. She says that the accord's defeat does not signal the end of debate over a new constitution for Canada. In native societies, she says, people "talk until the talking is done." Canada still has unfinished business. "How do you build a constitution," Norton asks, as she observes that European settlers of the United States "borrowed from the philosophy and principles of the Great Law of the Iroquois Confederacy." This gave them a connection to their new home. "Now," says Norton, "They are ready for the next step -- moving from principle to practice and respect for the First Peoples." This is one of several pieces of commentary on the "influence" issue to surface during Canada's constitutional debate.

1992.067. Wandell, Grace and Jack. "Viewpoint: Native Americans Have Rich Lore." Albany *Times-Union*, March 31, 1992, p. A-10.

The authors critique a commentary on CBS' "Sixty Minutes" by Andy Rooney, whose home town is Albany. In response to Rooney's assertion that Native American lifestyles are "an anachronism," the Wandells list contributions of a material and intellectual nature, including an observation that "the...Haudenosaunee institution of government was surely one of the key factors contributing to the form of modern American republics."

1992.068. White, Timothy. "Native American Song, Then and Now." *Billboard*, May 9, 1992, p. 5.

This piece in the large-circulation entertainment industry trade organ *Billboard* discusses the music of John Trudell, a Santee Sioux who was one of the founders of the American Indian Movement, particularly his collection "AKA Graffiti Man." As part of his article, White briefly summarizes Native American contributions to general American society, including foods and medicines, citing Weatherford, *Indian Givers* [1988]. White writes: "Even our Founding Fathers' concepts for governing the wilderness settlements were shaped by the Iroquois Confederacy's Great Law of Peace...."

1992.069. Wittstock, Laura Waterman. "A Good Ol' (Native) American Civics Test." *Fellowship*, September, 1992, pp. 9, 17.

Donald A. Grinde, Jr. comments on Native American contributions to democracy, one aspect of history that the magazine thought it subscribers "should know before the Columbus Quincentennial year is over."

Video

1992.070. Oren Lyons, [Onondaga member of the Iroquois Grand Council], "Bill Moyers' Journal" [Public Broadcasting Service], July 4, 1992.

Lyons discussed Iroquois ecological and political traditions, and asserted Iroquoian precedents for United States government. Lyons also illustrated the interview with some of his own artwork, as well as pieces by John Kahionhes Fadden that he created for *Exemplar of Liberty* [1991]. The program was shown on the United States' Independence Day. In a similar vein, Lyons appeared a year later on "Larry King Live."

Speech Transcript

1992.071. Transcript, "Notes for a Speech by the Right Honorable Joe Clark...President of the Privy Council and Minister Responsible for Constitutional Affairs." [At the annual meeting of the Canadian Manufacturer's Association] Toronto, June 12, 1992. In LEXIS.

Clark addresses the problems of Canadian nationhood as it impinges on the present constitutional debate in that country. Clark asserts the right and ability of Native Canadians to govern themselves, pointing to the Iroquois: "Aboriginal self-government...was here when Thomas Jefferson and Benjamin Franklin looked to the Iroquois Confederacy when they were designing the American Constitution." As president of the Privy Council and Minister Responsible for Constitutional Affairs, Clark was the top-ranking public official in Canada's debate over a new constitution.

1991

Books, Scholarly and Specialty Journals

1991.001. Berger, Thomas R. *A Long and Terrible Shadow: White Values, Native Rights in the Americas, 1492-1992.* Vancouver, B.C.: Douglas & MacIntyre, 1991.

Berger, a lawyer and a former justice of the British Columbia Supreme Court, writes (on page 58) of the Iroquois Confederacy's political system, and observes that "The Europeans, especially the English, were undoubtedly impressed by its sophistication." Berger cites *Forgotten Founders* [1982,1987] in this regard, and says "This is not an idiosyncratic view. Many historians, including Henry Steele Commager, have acknowledged the contribution of Iroquois political ideas to the political thought of the Founding Fathers, especially Benjamin Franklin."

1991.002. D'Souza, Dinesh. *Illiberal Education: The Politics of Race and Sex on Campus.* New York: The Free Press, 1991.

On page 75, D'Souza derides the contents of *Multicultural Literacy* [See Simonson, 1988] as ignoring "the literary classics of Asia and the Middle East." Instead, writes D'Souza, the anthology, which has been widely adopted as a text in multicultural education, publishes "thirteen essays of protest." D'Souza names two of them, including Paula Gunn Allen's "The Red Roots of White Feminism." Following this piece, D'Souza became a frequent critic of the "influence" thesis without ever realizing that an academic debate was going on. See his best-selling polemic *The End of Racism* [1995].

1991.003. Foner, Eric and John A. Garraty, eds. *The Reader's Companion to American History.* Boston: Houghton-Mifflin, 1991.

On page 551, as part of a discussion of warfare in the Northeast during the early years of European colonization, this encyclopedic-type work mentions the Iroquois League, which, for two centuries, "was able to withstand the efforts of Europeans to seize their living space." A brief description of the Iroquois political structure follows, with this conclusion: "Long before the coming of Europeans, they had put together a federation (similar to the confederation that created the United States)."

1991.004. Grinde and Johansen. *Exemplar of Liberty: Native America and the Evolution of Democracy.* Los Angeles: UCLA American Indian Studies Center.

Published in December, *Exemplar of Liberty* follows the theme of Native Americans as examples of liberty from Roger Williams in the seventeenth century through the revolutionary, confederation, and Constitutional periods, into nineteenth-century reflections on the Iroquois in Lewis Henry Morgan, Karl Marx, Frederick Engels, Elizabeth Cady Stanton, and Matilda Joslyn Gage. This book contains bibliographic references on the idea to the year 1900, and so may be used to complement this bibliography.

1991.005. Hunter, Robert and Robert Calihoo. *Occupied Canada: A Young White Man Discovers His Unsuspected Past.* McClelland and Stewart, 1991.

Calihoo was raised in Edmonton under the name Robert Royer by a very proper but racist white grandmother. After her death, when he was 10 years of age, Calihoo calls on his father, Albert Calihoo, whom he had not previously met. He discovers that Albert is a Native American, a Mohawk, whose family hails from Kahnawake, near Montreal. Young Calihoo is introduced to reservation live and its privations as he discovers what Canada has done to the people whose identity he is now assuming. Part of the book is his biography; the rest, by professional writer Robert Hunter, is an expose of conditions faced by First Peoples in Canada. Hunter also surveys Native contributions to many cultures, including the impact of the Iroquois on the likes of Locke, Thoreau, Tolstoy, and, according to one reviewer, "their effect on American democracy, Marxist communism, the French revolution, and the Law of the Sea." In a chapter titled "The Great Gift of the Iroquois," (pp. 190-202) this book describes the operation of the Iroquois League and its impact on the developing United States and its founders extensively, quoting liberally from Johansen, *Forgotten Founders* [1982, 1987].

1991.006. Jacobs, Renee. "The Iroquois Great Law of Peace and the U.S. Constitution: How the Founding Fathers Ignored the Clan Mothers." *American Indian Law Review.* 16 (1991):497-531.

While the founders adapted some aspects of Iroquois law, Jacobs makes a strong case that they were nearly totally blind to the equity of the sexes that was woven into Haudenosaunee fundamental law and political life. Jacobs asks why the Founders were sensitive to some aspects of Iroquois law and not to others. She cites Sally Roesch Wagner's introduction to Matilda Joslyn Gage, *Woman, Church & State,* and *Forgotten Founders* [1982, 1987].

1991.007. Jensen, Erik M. "The Imaginary Connection Between the Great Law of Peace and the United States Constitution: A Reply to Professor Schaaf," *American Indian Law Review* 15:2 (1991), pp. 295-308.

See also: Schaaf, Gregory. "From the Great Law of Peace to the Constitution of the United States: A Revision of America's Democratic Roots." *American Indian Law Review* 14 (1989).

Jensen calls Schaaf's argument "one of the more extreme presentations of the idea" of Native American influence on American political theory and practice. Instead of presenting what Grinde calls a "mosaic of history," Schaaf places the Great Law and the Constitution side by side and draws what he believes to be parallels. Schaaf has contended that the Great Law was "the model" for the Constitution, and that the United States' founding document diverges from the Great Law only because the Founders did not go far enough to emulate the Iroquois model.

Jensen comments on page 297: "...[T]he time for Professor Schaaf's theory has not come and will not come -- if we care about historical truth. The proposition is nonsense...and recognized as such by nearly all serious historians." Jensen quotes Francis Jennings, commenting on a U.S. Senate resolution supporting the "influence thesis" (See 1987) as saying that the resolution "destroys my faith in the historical literacy of the Senate." (footnote 14, page 297) Jensen writes that Schaaf's work lacks primary documentation; "This proposition is grounded in quicksand."

(p. 301) Jensen does acknowledge that Founders such as Franklin and Jefferson discussed Indians copiously in their writings, and that their images of the Indians were factored into their view of natural rights. He rejects the native role in formulating governance, however: "A people considered to be without law and government, as the founders saw the Indians, can hardly be considered a model for the U.S. Constitution." (p. 304). He inclines toward the position that oral renditions of the Great Law may have adapted the language of the Constitution, rather than *vice versa*. Jensen also acknowledges the role of Iroquois philosophy in the development of Marxism, through Lewis Henry Morgan. He cites Grinde and Johansen's early works [1977, 1982], but does not analyze them.

1991.008. Johansen. "Back to the Future." *Native Nations* 1:4(1990), pp. 16-17, 32.

Review of Jack Weatherford's *Indian Givers* and *Native Roots*.

1991.009. Johansen. "Native American Societies and the Evolution of Political Thought in the United States." *Akwesasne Notes* 22:5 (December-January, 1990-91), pp. 7-9.

Written text of a presentation delivered at the University of South Dakota, October, 1988.

1991.010. Johansen. "Native American Roots for Freedom of Expression as a Form of Liberty." *Journal of Communication Inquiry*, 15:2(Summer, 1991), pp. 48-69.

Excerpts from *Exemplar of Liberty* [1991] describing some Founders' (especially Benjamin Franklin and Thomas Jefferson's) observations of Native American societies on the subjects of liberty, freedom of speech, *et al.*

1991.011. Mander, Jerry. *In the Absence of the Sacred.* San Francisco: Sierra Club Books, 1991.

In the Absence of the Sacred calls for a return to a sense of sacredness of the earth expressed in many American Indian religious philosophies as an alternative to "technoutopian" thinking which has created an economic system that is devouring the last indigenous niches of the earth, and polluting the entire planet. At a time when toxic levels of PCBs have been found in Inuit (Eskimo) mothers' milk thousands of miles from their sources, Mander calls for a revolution in philosophy and economics. The book surveys Native American history in North America, including the Iroquois League; the author says that the discovery that Native Americans helped shape democratic thought was his most exciting while researching the book. In his rush to embrace the idea, Mander makes several minor factual errors.

1991.012. Moynihan, Daniel Patrick. *The American Indian*. New York: Chelsea House, 1991.

This is a brief survey of American Indian cultures and history introduced by Senator Moynihan. the text itself carries no personal credit. On pp. 55-57, the book briefly discusses the Iroquois and their Great Law of Peace. "Some contemporary Iroquois believe that several aspects of their society were incorporated by the Founding Fathers into the Constitution of the new American nation. They are quick to point out ways in which they were more democratic than the citizens of...Rome and Greece." (p. 57)

1991.013. Waldman, Carl. *Who Was Who in Native American History*. New York: Facts on File, 1990.

In his entry on Benjamin Franklin, Waldman notes (on page 123) that "Franklin helped draft the Declaration of Independence and organized the new American government, basing some political concepts, it has been suggested, on the Iroquois League of Six Nations."

Newspapers and Magazines

1991.014. Asimov, Nanette. "Multicultural Approach: History Rewritten for the New School Year," San Francisco *Chronicle*, September 3, 1991, p. A-1.

The article begins: "Historic changes are happening to history. As students return to public schools throughout California today, many will learn stories that they nor their parents have not heard before -- That an African doctor named Imhotep made significant contributions to medical knowledge 2,000 years before Hippocrates; that the framers of the U.S. Constitution studied the bylaws of the Iroquois nation...."

1991.015. Brett, Brian. Our History From a Native Point of View..." Vancouver *Sun*, August 17, 1991, p. D-19.

In this review of Robert Hunter and Robert Calihoo's *Occupied Canada*, Brett says that "The text oozes into the wild assertion that anarchism, communism, and modern democracy (tell that to the Greeks!) evolved directly from the Iroquois."

1991.016. Cronin, Mary Elizabeth. "Indian Influence on U.S. Founders." Seattle *Times*, May 17, 1991, p. B-2.

Report on a presentation by Grinde at the University of Washington (Bothell campus).

1991.017. Doyle, Leonard. "American War of Interdependence Breaks Out." *The Independent* [London], June 22, 1991, p. 1.

Doyle surveys debates over multicultural education in the United States, describing controversy attending the New York State Education Department's recent report "One Nation, Many Peoples: a Declaration of Cultural Interdependence." He writes, in part, that "pupils will learn that the American Constitution owes as much to the political system of the Iroquois Confederacy...as to European models."

1991.018. D'Souza, Dinesh. "The Visigoths in Tweed." *Forbes* [Cover Story, April 1, 1991, p. 81.

D'Souza, a research fellow at the American Enterprise Institute, targets "a new barbarism -- dogmatic, intolerant, and oppressive" that he says has "descended on America's institutions of higher learning...a neo-Marxist ideology promoted in the name of multiculturalism." He quotes William King, president of the Black Student Union at Stanford University, who cited a number of items of multicultural history before that school's Faculty Senate, including "that the Iroquois Indians in America had a representative democracy which served as a model for the American system."

1991.019. George, Douglas M. (Kanentiio). "Dancing With Myths." Washington *Post*, April 13, 1991, p. A-17.

George, editor of *Akwesasne Notes*, is replying to a piece by Paul W. Valentine [Hollywood's Noble Indians: Are We Dancing With Myths?" Washington *Post*, March 31, 1991]. George says Valentine argues that the movie "Dances With Wolves" stereotypes Indians as he uses stereotypes himself. According to George, Valentine also ignores "native achievements in architecture, political theory, and the arts." One such example of the rich history that Valentine ignores, says George, is "the democratic institutions created by the Iroquois, which formed, according to historian Donald Grinde, the basis for the U.S. system of government," including universal suffrage, a right not extended to women in the United States until 1919.

1991.020. Grenier, Richard. "Revisionists Adrift in a Sea of Ignorance." Washington *Times*, November 15, 1991, p. F-3.

Grenier is splitting a gut over multiculturalism. "New York State, as its official educational policy, now honors the Iroquois Nation as a prime cultural influence on American civilization....Why does the U.S. Constitution, on which the Iroquois are now credited with having a powerful influence, not provide for such well-established former Iroquois traditions as raiding and murder of rival tribesmen, old people, and children too small to be useful? Why doesn't it guarantee the right to rape..." Grenier says that the Indians cast in the movie *Black Robe* were "bracingly authentic." He defines "authentic" as "Dirty, cruel, they brutalize, [and] torture."

1991.021. Hilderbrand, John. "Rewriting History? School Panel Wrestles With Curriculum." *Newsday*, June 18, 1991, p. 5.

Hilderbrand describes New York State proposals to change the teaching of social studies in its public schools which are being accused of comprising "ethnic cheerleading." Among specific issues that he cites as being involved in this debate is "Was the U.S. Constitution inspired by the earlier Iroquois government?"

1991.022. Hildebrand. "Iroquois Stake Claim to Constitution." *Newsday*, June 18, 1991.

1991.023. Holt, Patricia. "Technology on Trial..." [Review of Mander, *In the Absence of* the Sacred] San Francisco *Chronicle*, November 17, 1991, p. 1 [Sunday Review].

The reviewer calls the Iroquois "our true founding fathers...whose Great Law offered a model for democracy."

1991.024. Holt, Patricia. "Indian Influences at America's Core." [Review of Weatherford, *Native Roots*] San Francisco *Chronicle*, December 25, 1991, p. E-8 [Books].

This is a review of *Native Roots*, as well as an interview with Jack Weatherford, "who believes...the big surprise of our history is that Indians...Americanized European settlers." In the arena of politics, says Weatherford, "The League of the Iroquois was Benjamin Franklin's model for parts of the Constitution."

1991.025. Hopkins, Anne and Daniel S. Levy. "Upside Down in the Groves of Academe." *Time*, April 1, 1991, pp. 66-69.

The article's focus is "political correctness." On page 67, the authors take up the "influence thesis" in this context: "In the nation's elementary and secondary schools, the polarization is not yet so extreme. But increasingly curriculums are being written to satisfy the demands of parents and community activists. In some cases, expediency counts for more than facts. New York State officials, for example, have responded to pressure from Native American leaders by revamping the state high school curriculum to include the shaky assertion that he U.S. Constitution was based on the political system of the Iroquois Confederacy." Like many opponents of this idea, the authors of this article overstate the thesis as they discredit it. [Files contain an unpublished letter from Johansen to the editors of *Time*, March 28, 1991.]

1991.026. Johansen. "The Search Goes on in America for Complete, Credible History." Omaha *World-Herald*, November 6, 1991, p. 27.

Rebuttal to George Will's syndicated column [below], addressing critics of "political correctness."

1991.027. Johnson, Christine. "Johansen's Book Credits Native Americans." University of Nebraska at Omaha *Gateway*, April 9, 1991, p. 10.

Report on presentation by Grinde and Johansen at UNO, April 4. Files contain an advertising flier for the event, prepared by Johansen.

1991.028. Kaminski, John. "U.S., Soviet Constitutions Stolen From the Iroquois: But Our Founding Fathers, Engels Bungled the Theft." *The New England Pilgrim*, 1:1(December, 1991), pp. 1, 8-9.

As the headline suggests, the lead story of the *Pilgrim's* first issue, written by its editor, is a sometimes hyperbolistic description in avid support of the idea that the Iroquois Great Law of Peace helped shape the founding documents of the United States. History indicates that the Great Law was freely offered to the colonists, so it couldn't have been "stolen."

1991.029. Lord, Lewis and Sarah Burke. "America Before Columbus." *U.S. News & World Report*, July 8, 1991, p. 2.

This cover story is a survey of Native American life before the arrival of Columbus. It says: "Three centuries before the U.S. Constitution took shape, the Iroquois League ran a Congress-like council, exercised the veto, protected freedom of speech, and let women choose officeholders...."

1991.030. Maracle, Brian. "Native History Uneasily Packages Two Books As One." Montreal *Gazette*, July 27, 1991, p. J-1.

Maracle, a Mohawk writer and broadcaster, says that Robert Hunter and Robert Calihoo's *Occupied Canada* [1991] is "part autobiography, part history, part diatribe and plea for justice, and, ultimately, [a] frustrating experience." The most satisfying chapters in the book, writes Maracle, contain its "searing assessment of Canada's treatment of native people," as well as work which details the Iroquois' influence on many philosophies around the world, including American democracy, Marxist communism, *et al.*

1991.031. Reich, Ernest J. "'Politically Correcting' History is Bad." [Letter to the editor] Orlando *Sentinel-Tribune*, September 13, 1991, p. A-18.

Borrowing from a column by George Will (see below), Reich picks up the anti-multiculturalist wail about students in New York State who are supposedly pressing their noses to the academic grindstone in pursuit of Iroquois influence on the Constitution. This writer puts the case even more crudely than Will: "A school system in New York State was blatantly teaching the falsehood that the development of the U.S. Constitution was directly influenced by the Iroquois Indians."

1991.032. Rohn, Elizabeth J. "Anti-Columbus Protestors Ignore Iroquois' Wishes." [Letter to the editor] Washington *Times*, October 25, 1991, p. F-2.

Following an act of vandalism against a statue of Columbus on Columbus Day, 1991, in Washington, D.C., Rohn notes that an Iroquois delegation planted a white pine tree in Constitution Park on September 17, 1988. She adds: "Some Native Americans believe this confederacy [the Iroquois] was the first form of representative government, and the idea was given to the Founding Fathers."

1991.033. Russell, George. "Reading, Writing -- and Iroquois Politics." *Time*, November 11, 1991, pp. 20-22.

Interview with New York Commissioner of Education Thomas Sobol. In response to a question about the "influence thesis," Sobol replied: "Well, it depends on the way we teach it. It's very clear to me that our Constitution derives from the political traditions and thinking of Western Europe. Now it is a fact, I guess, that the Iroquois nations learned to live compatibly with one another. Whether or not they had any impact on the framers of the Constitution, I don't know, but I am set to acknowledge its possible influence in part. It makes sense to me not to overemphasize it." The interviewer then asked, "Why teach it at all?" Sobol replied: "Why teach anything that's part of our history if there's only a few people involved. Why would you want *not* to teach it?...There's no harm in talking about it."

1991.034. Seneca, Martin W. "Adrift in a Sea of Ignorance? Indians Deserve the Last Word." Washington *Times*, November 24, 1991, p. B-5.

Seneca, who lives on the Cattaraugus reservation, is replying to a column [above] by Richard Grenier (November 15) that held the Iroquois to be primitive, violent, and ignorant. Referring to the influence of the Iroquois political model on the United States, Seneca writes: "This powerful Iroquois influence was known even...in 1776 when Benjamin Franklin was drafting the Constitution [Articles of Confederation]....Any articulate historian, honest and unbiased, should not have to ask about Iroquois influence. We are well-documented on this."

1991.035. Starna, William A. "Iroquois Constitutional Influence?" Letter to the Editor, *Time*, December 2, 1991, p. 10.

Starna, responding to a *Time* interview with New York Commissioner of Education Thomas Sobol [Nov. 11], says that he and other university-based non-Native American academics reviewed *Haudenosaunee: Past, Present, Future,* and found "no good evidence" to support "Iroquois impact on the framers of the Constitution." "Years of research by non-conspiratorial scholars" has disproved the idea, Starna asserts; "No informed historian makes this argument."

1991.036. Stewart, Edison. "Grant Natives 'Real Power,' Clark Says." Toronto *Star*, September 10, 1991, p. A-13.

Constitutional Affairs Minister Joe Clark says that the recognition of natives' right to govern themselves is "no less fundamental than the recognition of Quebec as a distinct society." In a speech at Queen's University in Kingston, Ontario, attended by a standing-room only crowd, Clark said that both issues "will determine whether this country will succeed or fail." To support his contention that aboriginal people should govern themselves, he said, according to this account, that "elaborate and sophisticated systems of native self-government existed long before European settlers arrived. The Iroquois Confederacy, for example, was a model for the American constitution."

1991.037. Weatherford, Jack. "A Year to Discover Rich History of the Very First Americans." Minneapolis *Star-Tribune*, October 13, 1991, p. 21-A.

"In the realm of politics, the Indians not only gave us the word 'caucus,' but they taught us how to make a caucus, and from this developed a major part of our political system and the convention system by which we nominate presidential candidates. Other parts of Indian political institutions were incorporated into the constitution, including impeachment of elected officials, the separation of military and civilian personnel, and the admission of new states as equal members into the union."

1991.038. Will, George. "Therapeutic History is Snake Oil," syndicated column [Washington Post Writers Group] in Seattle *Post-Intelligencer*, July 14, 1991.

Will, writing about "feel-good history," brings the New York State curriculum guide into his argument as an example. Referring to references in the guide to Iroquois contributions to the Constitution, Will says: "Such fictions are supposed to nurture minorities' 'self-esteem'...on the basis of scant evidence." This was the second of three times that Will derided the "influence" issue in his column between 1989 and 1993, with no inkling that a scholarly debate was going on regarding it. He cites no sources, and appears unaware that a literature exists on the subject.

1991.039. Wisneski, Richard. "Indian Says Environment Important Heritage." Plattsburgh *Press-Republican*, n.d.

Interview with Ray Fadden: "...[T]he Declaration of Independence was based on the Indian system of government. Thomas Jefferson said this himself. The ideas of democracy, freedom and tolerance are more Indian than European."

1991.040. Witham, Larry. "Indians' Political Muscle Flexed Over Past 20 Years." Washington *Times*, July 23, 1991, p. A-5.

A speculation presented in a letter by William A. Starna appears again as fact in this news article. During the debate over the New York State "Curriculum of Inclusion," Starna expressed a fear that he would be "blacklisted" (his word) from doing anthropological work on Iroquois reservations. He presented no evidence to substantiate this fear. Nevertheless, in this article, we are told that "Indian leaders blacklisted anthropologist William A. Starna for rejecting the idea that the U. S. Constitution was based on the Iroquois federation." The author of this piece also asserts that "some Indians [are] beating an ideological drum by calling America's European heritage into question or making unreasonable claims." He does not specify who is making the assertions, or what is being claimed (not to mention whom "blacklisted" Starna).

School Workbook

1991.041. Jan Maher and Doug Selwyn, *Native Americans: Grades 3 and 4.* Seattle: Turman Publishing, 1991.

Pages 15-16 discuss the Iroquois Great Law of Peace, Benjamin Franklin's use of it in the Albany Plan, and the writing of the Constitution. This is an elementary school workbook.

1990

Books, Scholarly and Specialty Journals

1990.001. Clifton, James. *The Invented Indian: Cultural Fictions and Government Policies.* New Brunswick, N.J.: Transaction Publishers, 1990.

American Indians had no environmental ethic, had few notions of political equality, and had nothing to do with the development of democracy. Meet the "Indian" as invented by James Clifton, who labels even James Axtell as an Indiansymp (p. 41). On pages 25 and 26, Clifton begins this book of essays by various authors by whining that Indians will use the approaching anniversary of Columbus' first landings as an excuse to indulge in "victimization" through such "in-house journals" as *Northeast Indian Quarterly* and the *American Indian Culture & Research Journal*. Clifton takes aim at Weatherford's *Indian* Givers [1988], and at Vine Deloria, Jr., whom, he predicts, "will publish a book titled, *Columbus Was Red*." (p. 26) This book also contains an abridged version of Elisabeth Tooker's 1988 *Ethnohistory* article "The U.S. Constitution and the Iroquois League," on pp. 107-128. For reaction, see Deloria [1992] and Churchill [1992].

1990.002. Johansen, Bruce E. and Donald A. Grinde, Jr. "The Debate Regarding Native American Precedents for Democracy: A Recent Historiography." *American Indian Culture & Research Journal* 14:1 (Summer, 1990), pp. 61-88.

Survey of the debate over the "influence" issue to the end of 1989.

1990.003. Johansen, "Native American Societies and the Evolution of Democracy in America, 1600-1800." *Ethnohistory* 37:3(Summer, 1990), pp. 279-290.

Rebuttal to Elisabeth Tooker's "U.S. Constitution and the Iroquois League," in *Ethnohistory* [1988].

1990.004. Lowi, Theodore J. and Benjamin Ginsberg. *American Government: Freedom and Power*. New York: W. W. Norton & Co., 1990.

Page 68 of this textbook contains a sidebar ("Box 3.1") titled "The Iroquois League: Native American Model." The text briefly outlines the origins and nature of the Iroquois League, and says that "at least one clear link" indicates that Iroquois ideas were incorporated into Euroamerican political philosophy -- the 1754 Albany conference and Franklin's Albany Plan. Ironically, the authors' major cited source is Elisabeth Tooker's essay on the Iroquois in *The Handbook of North*

American Indians, Vol. 15, ed. Bruce G. Trigger [Washington, D.C.: Smithsonian Institution, 1978, pp. 418-441]. The discussion in this textbook is marred by a mangled spelling of "Seneca" (as "Secca").

1990.005 McGaa, Ed. *Mother Earth Spirituality*. San Francisco: Harper, 1990.

In Chapter 3 ("Pilgrims, Founding Fathers, and Indians"), McGaa briefly describes Cannassatego's advice to the colonists (1744), Benjamin Franklin's use of Iroquois models in the Albany Plan (1754), and the Founders' use of federalism similar to the Iroquois. The book cites *Forgotten Founders* [1982, 1987].

1990.006. Nollman, Jim. *Spiritual Ecology: A Guide to Reconnecting With Nature*. New York: Bantam, 1990.

On page 13, in the context of describing the Iroquois belief in decision-making for the seventh generation to come, Nollman writes: "Thomas Jefferson was said to have drawn much inspiration from the structure of Iroquois democracy in the process of blueprinting our American system of government....How would our lives be different today if Jefferson had included the rights of the seventh generation in the Bill of Rights?"

1990.007. Tooker, Elisabeth, "Rejoinder to Johansen." *Ethnohistory* 37:3 (Summer, 1990), pp. 291-297.

1990.008. Yarrow, David. *The Dragon and the Ice Castle: Rediscovery of Sacred Space in the Finger Lakes*. Charlottesville, VA: Solstice, circa 1990.

Yarrow's examination of Upstate New York "sacred space" includes a brief account of the Iroquois Confederacy's founding epic, and refers to Iroquois attendance at debates which shaped the Declaration of Independence in the spring of 1776.

Newspapers and Magazines

1990.009. _____. "Interior Kicks Off Indian Month Celebration." *Indian News: Week in Review*.

Vol. 14, No. 13. Washington, D.C.: Department of Interior, Bureau of Indian Affairs. November 2, 1990, p. 2.

Interior secretary Manuel Lujan observed National Indian Heritage Month with an address November 1 in the South Interior Auditorium, Washington, D.C. His address included material contributions to American culture by Native Americans. On the subject of intellectual contributions, Lujan said: "...When it came time to set up a government that has lasted for more than 200 years, we did not hesitate to borrow in part from a pattern that was working well for the Iroquois Nation."

1990.010. Berger, Joseph. "Now the Regents Must Decide if History Will be Recast," New York *Times* [Week in Review], Feb. 11, 1990.

See Starna, William A., letter to New York *Times*, March 7, 1990, below.

1990.011. Fadden, John Kahionhes. "Democracy," Letter to the Editor, Massena [New York] *Daily Courier-Observer*, November 3, 1990.

Cites from *Exemplar of Liberty* and other books, as well as Iroquois oral history, to support the influence thesis. Fadden, a Mohawk, created line drawings for *Exemplar*, and was reading early drafts of the manuscript at this time.

1990.012. Gastil, Raymond D. "What Kind of Democracy." *The Atlantic*, June, 1990, p. 92.

Gastil surveys roots of democracy worldwide in his search for definitions that fit conditions in today's world. In his survey (much as John Adams did in his *Defence of the Constitutions...*), Gastil includes the Iroquois Confederacy, along with European precedents such as the Swiss cantons, the Dutch republic, and provisions of English common law.

1990.013. Grenier, Richard. "Historic Identity Crises." Washington *Times*, March 27, 1990, p. F-3.

Grenier spars with notions of multicultural education, including: "African-Americans claim that Queen Nefertiti of ancient Egypt was black. Iroquois Indians have induced New York State education officials to include in their 11th-grade syllabus the dogmatic assertion that the Iroquois Confederacy was a major influence on the U.S. Constitution." He labels such assertions unfactual, and racist. If the Iroquois can claim to have influenced the Constitution, then people of Mongolian descent have the right to insist that Genghis Khan "was a principal influence on the United States Constitution." Grenier is a columnist for The Washington *Times*.

1990.014. Grenier, Richard. "The New Treason of the Clerks: Criticism of American Liberal Intellectuals." *National Review* 42:14 (July 23, 1990), p. 42.

Grenier takes aim at a speech by Czechoslovakia's president Vaclav Havel that urged American academics to become more politically involved. Grenier replies that on American university campuses, "a new breed of treasonous clerks has emerged" who express "hostility to the ideals that underlie American democratic institutions [which] has become both blatant and grotesque." The "treason" is that standard European-derived fare in humanities departments now faces competition from "a hodgepodge of world cultures." First on Grenier's list of such transgressions is "the constitutional principles of the Iroquois."

1990.015. Hart, Jeffrey. "Japan to the Rescue: Japanese Higher Education." *National Review*, May 28, 1990, p. 39.

Hart asserts that the Japanese are becoming more "Eurocentric" as many people in the United States advocate becoming more "multicultural." As an example of this trend, he takes up the New York State "Curriculum of Inclusion," which he says "tells minorities that the Iroquois Indians contributed to the political theory of the U.S. Constitution. That's right. Lies will make us free."

1990.016. Hendricks, Mike. "Does Constitution Copy Confederacy?" Associated Press in Syracuse *Herald-American*, July 18, 1990.

This newspaper wire story quotes Donald A. Grinde, Jr. regarding attendance of Iroquois at debates over the Declaration of Independence, as well as references to the Iroquois government in John Adams' *Defence of the Constitutions....* Also describes native concepts of federalism. Rebuttal by Jan Wojcik, humanities professor at Clarkson University, Potsdam, New York, who is quoted as saying "The evidence is flimsy at best....[Franklin] was contemptuous of the Iroquois and referred to them as savages."

1990.017. House, Billy. "Regents Tackle Social Studies." Gannett News Service, Feb. 16, 1990.

This is a discussion of New York State's "Curriculum of Inclusion," and the debate over its multicultural emphasis. Speaking of prior curricula, House says that "Word that a democracy existed in New York state centuries before patriots convened in Philadelphia might not have gotten...to classrooms." The article quotes State School Chancellor Martin Barrell as he "rattled off dozens of examples that he said showed that blacks, Latins, Indians, Asians, and others have not been given their due in U.S. history....Among them, Barrell noted that a democracy was in place in New York state in the form of the six-nation Iroquois (or Haudenosaunee) Confederacy long before the arrival of Europeans."

1990.018. Johnson, Margaret. "A Historic Year." St. Louis *Post-Dispatch*, January 1, 1990, p. 2-B.

The author is taking issue with George Will's characterization of multicultural education. She applauds the day when school curricula will be purged of Eurocentric bias, "and the Iroquois people are honored for the ideas of our Constitution as...[it] is based on the constitution of the Iroquois nation, one of the Native American civilizations that the white European invaders systematically destroyed."

1990.019. Jones, Clive. "Two Founding Peoples Ignore the Aboriginals." [Letter to the editor] Toronto *Star*, August 20, 1990, p. A-14.

Jones criticizes the idea that Canada has "two founding peoples" -- the French and the English. The Canadian constitution and school textbooks ignore the rights of "our true founding peoples -- the aboriginal nation[s] of this continent," he asserts, adding: "Do most

Canadians realize that the constitution of the Iroquois Confederacy (a sophisticated system of checks and balances to ensure peace and stability) predates our own by a matter of some 850 years?"

1990.020. Leo, John. "A Fringe History of the World." *U.S. News & World Report*, November 12, 1990, pp. 25-26.

Leo assails "multiculturalism" in school curricula, beginning with "afrocentric" ideas, continuing (on page 26) to the *Haudenosaunee* curriculum in New York State. Leo hews to the "party line" of the curriculum's opponents, who assert that the influence of the Iroquois on American statecraft was included only to appease the Iroquois, not because it was part of history. "In Upstate New York, a Native American lobby demonstrated how a curriculum can now be altered by adroit special pleading. After a visit by an Iroquois delegation to the state education department, the school curriculum was amended to say that the political system of the Iroquois Confederacy influenced the writing of the U.S. Constitution."

[The meeting with State Education Department officials at which Iroquois "lobbyists" were said to have pressured the New York Education Department never occurred. Files (1992) contain a letter from John Kahionhes Fadden to Johansen, which says, in part: "For what it's worth on the debate issue...the idea for it was not the result of 'lobbying' by the Iroquois as some of the detractors have written. The idea for the guide was brought up at a meeting at SED. The meeting resulted from a letter-writing campaign directed toward inaccuracies in a specific field-test draft, *Social Studies 7 & 8: United States and New York State History*. During that January 8, 1987 meeting the concept of a curriculum guide was suggested by Donald H. Bragaw, chief, Bureau of Social Studies Education, and was supported by Ed Lalor, director, Division of Program Planning. The idea *did not* emanate from the Haudenosaunee 'lobbyists' who were there to address the draft mentioned above." Emphasis in original.]

Leo then writes: "The idea that the Founding Fathers borrowed from the Iroquois is a century-old myth. No good evidence exists to support it. [Here Leo quotes Starna's earlier letter to the New York *Times* without crediting him.] But it is now official teaching in New York State. [It wasn't. It was part of a curriculum under development.] To the surprise of very few, this decision shows that some school authorities, eager to avoid minority-group pressure and rage, are now willing to treat the curriculum as a prize in an ethnic spoils system."

Leo's essay very concisely sums up the argument of "influence thesis" opponents: The idea is "fiction." "idiocy," a "hoax," or "a myth," that is being imposed on innocent school children by a small group of somehow awesomely powerful, media-hungry Iroquois who want to muscle this falsehood into "mainstream" history. Like Will, Grenier, Buchanan, and others, Leo gives no hint that a scholarly debate is going on here. To suggest that the idea is even debatable (and not pure fiction, "myth," or "the silliest idea I've ever heard") would undermine the assumptions that fuel the arguments of Leo, Starna, Will, Tooker, *et al.*

1990.021. Morocco, Maria. "Indians Reclaim Legal History." *American Bar Association Journal*, August 6, 1990, p. 5.

This article describes a panel on Native American democracy at the 1990 convention of the American Bar Association in Chicago. The August 4 panel included Oren Lyons (Onondaga) Kirke Kickingbird (Kickapoo) Grinde (Yamasee), Johansen, and Judge Charles Cloud (Cherokee). The *ABA Journal* was the daily newspaper of the convention, which attracted about 20,000 people, the largest assembly of a professional organization in the world.

1990.022. New York *Post*. "The Sobol-Jeffries Victory." [Editorial], May 14, 1990.

This is the gutterball version of Starna's earlier letter to the New York *Times* [see below]. This editorial takes issue with Commissioner Sobol's decision, with a supporting vote from the state board of regents, to implement the "Curriculum of Inclusion" in New York schools. The editorial includes four subheads in bold-faced type: "WIDE CONDEMNATION," "BIZARRE PRIORITIES," "WASTING OUR MONEY," and "SELF-ESTEEM PABULUM." On the subject of the Iroquois and the development of democracy, it says: "In one unit, students are taught that an obscure Indian tribe in upper New York state was in great part responsible for the ideas that underlie the United States Constitution. This, of course, is utter nonsense."

1990.023. Ringwald, Christopher. "Ancient Teachings Inspire His Life." Albany *Times Union*, April 9, 1990.

As part of a series on the Iroquois, this interview with Tadadaho Leon Shenandoah takes up the influence issue: "Shenandoah repeated a belief common among Iroquois and some historians that the confederacy and its Great Law of Peace served as models for the U.S. Constitution. 'But they left out parts -- they did not bury their weapons, and they left out the religious,' he said. 'If they had included those, it would have been a different world.' He also faulted Western culture for its ceaseless striving. 'Everything in our way of life is giving thanks....The white man is never satisfied with creation, but wants to do better.'"

1990.024. Shepard, Daniel. "Native American Women: Real Symbol of Freedom," University of Nebraska at Omaha *Gateway*, March 20, 1990, p. 4.

Report on presentation at UNO March 12 by Sally Roesch Wagner and Johansen. Wagner spoke on ways in which the Iroquois and other Native Americans shaped nineteenth century feminism; Johansen spoke on the Indian image in the artwork of the American Revolution, including the use of an American Indian woman as a national symbol in revolutionary propaganda.

1990.025. Starna, William A. "Whose History Will be Taught, and What is History Anyway?" [Letter to the editor] New York *Times*, March 7, 1990.

Starna is responding to an article in the *Times* ["Now the Regents Must Decide," Week in Review, Feb. 11, 1990] which quotes Diane Ravitch as saying that the New York curriculum is "perhaps the only one in the nation" which incorporates the idea that the Iroquois helped shape the Constitution, and that this role was included "after an Iroquois delegation met with the State Education Department." Starna alleges that "some of the native writers and their Iroquois allies" have threatened to restrict access to Indian communities for Starna and others who criticize the *Haudenosaunee* curriculum guide in an apparent attempt to end their careers as "experts" on the Iroquois. Starna provides no specific proof of such threats. "No good evidence exists" to support the "influence" thesis, he maintains.

1990.026. Wood, Nancy. "Clashing Views Over Sovereignty." *Maclean's*, September 10, 1990, p. 18.

In this cover story for the Canadian newsmagazine *Maclean's*, Nancy Wood looks at the issue of Native American sovereignty in Canada, a very big issue in that country because of the confrontation at Oka, Quebec, which was continuing as this edition of *Maclean's* went to press. Wood asserts that the Mohawks and other Iroquois have given much evidence of an ability to govern themselves: "Mohawk history is replete with evidence of a sophisticated and deeply rooted political system...that predated European democracies by centuries." This coverage was centered around the crisis at Oka (Kanesatake), Quebec.

1989

Books, Scholarly and Specialty Journals

1989.001. _____. "Williamsburg Conference[:] Anthropologists Challenge Confederacy." *Akwesasne Notes* 21:2 (Spring, 1989), p. 18.

Report on the 1988 annual meeting of the American Society for Ethnohistory at Williamsburg, VA. The conference included a panel, "The Enduring Iroquois," at which Elisabeth Tooker presented a paper based on her 1988 article in *Ethnohistory* [below]. Grinde was listed as a discussant for this panel on the conference's preliminary program, but was deleted after conference organizer James Axtell said he could not find Grinde (who was doing research in the Washington, D.C. area) to confirm. [Files contain a copy of the 1988 ASE preliminary program listing Grinde, and the final program without him.] This report says that William N. Fenton "argued that no one in the British colonies in North America understood the Iroquois Confederacy....'Not until [Lewis] Henry Morgan did we understand the Confederacy,'" Fenton is quoted as saying.

Tooker is reported to have discussed Grinde's *Iroquois and the Founding of the American Nation* [1977] and Johansen's *Forgotten Founders* [1982]. She said that Grinde's book contained only three primary references, and that Johansen's was "of poor quality." "No serious scholar believes that the Iroquois influenced the U.S. government," Tooker said. "Only the bicentennial of the Constitution has brought attention to this." The second half of the report details ways in which "Iroquois experts" who discount native influence on democracy also oppose the *Haudenosaunee* curriculum guide, as well as return to the Iroquois of wampum belts held by New York State. Axtell later invited Grinde to organize a panel at the next year's ASE convention. The panel was organized and held in November, 1989 at Chicago. Grinde, Johansen, Tooker, and Sally Roesch Wagner appeared on the panel, with Fenton, Starna, and other critics of the "influence" thesis in the audience. This discussion is summarized in Johansen and Grinde, "Recent Historiography" [1990].

1989.002. Burton, Bruce A. "Squanto's Legacy: the Origin of the Town Meeting." *Northeast Indian Quarterly* 6:4(Winter, 1989), pp. 4-9.

Burton extends the "influence thesis" to early contacts between Europeans and Native Americans in New England, with particular attention to the origins of the traditional New England "town meeting" form of governance.

1989.003. Clay, Jason W. "Radios in the Rainforest..." *Technology Review*, October, 1989, p. 52.

This 2,800-word article describes ways in which aboriginal peoples around the world are using the tools of modern technology to enhance traditional cultures. Clay, an anthropologist, is director of research and publications at Cultural Survival; *Technology Review* is published at the Massachusetts Institute of Technology. The author says that "great advances in civilization have come not from the elimination of groups, but from interaction between cultures." As examples, he offers the fact that "Base 10" arithmetic spread from the Middle East to Europe, and "the organization of the League of the Iroquois had a profound effect on the forming of the U.S. Constitution, which is arguably one of the most influential documents ever written."

1989.004. Clifton, James A. *Being and Becoming Indian: Biographical Studies of North American Frontiers.* Chicago: The Dorsey Press, 1989.

This book of essays by different authors, similar in format to Clifton's *The Invented Indian* [1990] addresses the "influence thesis" in Chapter 1, "Alternate Identities and Cultural Frontiers," by Professor Clifton. On page 2, he refers to the U.S. Senate resolution enunciating Iroquois contributions to American government as a "bizarre revision of history," in response to "a skillful pressure campaign by the national Indian-rights lobby." Clifton then goes on to say that another "politically useful fable" is the environmental nature of Chief Seath'l's [whom Clifton anglicizes as "Seattle"] farewell speech. Those awesomely influential Iroquois have been at it again, feeding a gullible public lies about history, according to Clifton. As for his version of reality, if Native Americans want to claim historical credit for something, there's always scalping.

1989.005. Garon, Ross. "Pow Wow! Native American Indians' Contributions to Society." *Scholastic Update*, May 26, 1989, p. 4.

This piece surveys material and intellectual contributions of American Indians to American society generally. The Iroquois Confederacy is described briefly, as well as the effect it had on Benjamin Franklin from the Albany Plan to the Constitutional Convention.

1989.006. Grinde, Donald A., Jr. "Iroquoian Political Concept and the Genesis of American Government: Further Research and Contentions." *Northeast Indian Quarterly* 6:4(Winter, 1989), pp. 10-21.

Excerpts from Grinde and Johansen, *Exemplar of Liberty* [1991] as a work in progress. Grinde's concentration here is on the formation of the United States polity during the Constitutional era, including John Adams' critique of proposals by Benjamin Franklin for a single-house legislature.

1989.007. Hieronimus, Robert. *America's Secret Destiny: Spiritual Vision and the Founding of a Nation.* Rochester, Vt.: Destiny Books, 1989.

This "new-age" history brings the Iroquois contribution into its ambit in its first chapter (pp. 5-13). It notes Cannassatego's 1744 speech and Franklin's popularization of it, from *Forgotten Founders* [1982, 1987].

1989.008. Johansen, Bruce E. "William James Sidis' Tribes and States: An Unpublished Exploration of Native American Contributions to Democracy." *Northeast Indian Quarterly* Spring/Summer 1989, pp. 16-20.

In 1914, the child prodigy William James Sidis became he youngest person (at age 16) to graduate from Harvard. Much later press coverage of Sidis' life stresses the theme that he failed to fulfill his childhood promise. Sidis loathed publicity, and kept secret the fact that he was writing an 800-page history of the United States through the eyes of its original inhabitants. The second half of this unpublished manuscript has been lost. Done without standard scholarly annotation, Sidis' history describes native forms of governance at length, and argues that the the Penacook Confederacy was more democratic than the Iroquois, whom Sidis describes as oligarchic.

1989.009. Johansen. "Debate: Indians & Democracy." *Akwesasne Notes* 21:2 (Spring, 1989), pp. 19-20, 23.

An early version of the commentary on the debate later published by Johansen and Grinde in the *American Indian Culture & Research Journal* [1990]. Johansen described the use of Native American concepts in the writings of Benjamin Franklin and Thomas Jefferson, as well as Paul Revere's engravings during the revolutionary era that used an American Indian woman as a national symbol for the new United States.

1989.010. Marcus, Robert D. and David Burner. *America Firsthand: Readings in American History.* *Volume 1: From Settlement to Reconstruction.* New York: St, Martin's Press, 1989.

This book of historical readings includes one from Elias Johnson, a Tuscarora sachem. The preface to Johnson's statement (on page 9) considers that "When the first European settlers reached North America, they encountered people who themselves had complex values and traditions." The authors cite the Iroquois Confederacy as an example, and go on to say that it was able to create an effective confederacy without sacrificing tribal autonomy. "The American republic would wrestle with a similar problem, as Benjamin Franklin foresaw. Franklin, in fact, was so impressed with the structure of the Iroquois Confederacy that he recommended its government as a model for the colonies to join separate sovereign states into a powerful union."

1989.011. Seaborne, Adrian and David Evans. *Canada and its Pacific Neighbours.* Edmonton, Alberta: Weigl Educational Publishers Ltd., 1989.

In this social-studies textbook for middle-school students, the Great Law of Peace and the U.S. Constitution are compared in a box on page 154. The text quotes Cannassatego's speech at Lancaster on July 4, 1744, during which the Onondaga sachem advised British colonists to unite on an Iroquois model. On page 161, the Iroquois League is listed as one of five "Major World Peacekeeping Organizations and Agreements," with Pax Romana, the Geneva Convention, the League of Nations, and the United Nations. On page 173, the authors quote from the Great Law of Peace and the Constitution of the United Nations to show similarity. The book cites *Forgotten Founders*.

1989.012. Stineback, David. Review of *Forgotten Founders* [1982, 1987] in *American Indian Quarterly* (spring, 1989), pp. 192-194.

Although this is a book "I wish I could praise....It reads like the dissertation it once was," and too little attention is paid to Indian cultures and religious practices. "This does not mean that Johansen is wrong when he argues that 'the Enlightenment mind absorbed Indian tradition and myth,' or that Franklin in particular was extremely impressed by Iroquoian politics." (p. 193). The book is "an adequate beginning," Stineback concludes, but it lacks necessary background and systematic annotation.

1989.013. Venables, Robert W. "The Founding Fathers: Choosing to be the Romans." *Northeast Indian Quarterly* 6:4(Winter, 1989), pp. 30-55.

"Nearly two thousand years earlier, Roman legions had rolled over the tribal peoples of Northern Europe. In those Roman wars of conquest, the Founding Fathers' Northern European ancestors had played the role of Indians. This time, the Founding Fathers were determined to be the Romans." (p. 31) Venables asserts that the Founders borrowed from the Iroquois, *et al.*, out of their own self-interest in creating an empire. Land speculation by some of the Founders is detailed.

1989.014. Wagner, Sally Roesch. "The Root of Oppression is the Loss of Memory: The Iroquois and the Early Feminist Vision." *Akwesasne Notes* 21:1(Late winter, 1989), p. 11.

Wagner traces some of the ideology of Elizabeth Cady Stanton, Matilda Joslyn Gage, *et al.*, to their associations with Iroquois women during the mid-and-late nineteenth century. Wagner's work was a key source for Chapter 11 ("Persistence of an Idea") in *Exemplar of Liberty.*

Newspapers and Magazines

1989.015. _____. "How the Indians Solve Their Problems." *USA Today*, February 9, 1989, p. 8-A.

"Contrary to most movies and television, Indians have a proud history, not all primitive savagery. We borrowed from the Iroquois Confederation for our own Constitution. Today we can learn from the traditional Indian reverence for the land. We need to help preserve Indian culture."

1989.016. Bauer, Peter. "Adirondack Life Awards: Historic Preservation," *Adirondack Life*, Feb., 1989, pp. 60-62.

Award to Ray Fadden, for his replicated Iroquois story belts depicting life in the Iroquois Confederacy, "which has survived six centuries, despite brutal subjugation, to influence the thought and evolution of democracy....Only recently have these influences received critical examination from American scholars, who now recognize that the structure of the Iroquois Confederacy, with its elected representatives from each tribe to a high council, has shaped the U.S. Constitution as much as, if not more than, the writings of John Locke and Thomas Hobbes or the statutes of English common law."

1989.017. Beck, Barbara. "Tribal Pursuits: A Thanksgiving Tribute to Native Americans." Philadelphia *Daily News*, Nov. 24, 1989, p. 86.

"Some recent Native American literature tells us that Benjamin Franklin so admired the confederation of Indians in the Northeast that he used it as a model for the Constitution....Many colonists admired the Indians' respect for natural rights and their ideas of government....On May 1, 1779, the Continental Army celebrated St. Tammany's Day." A description of St. Tammany's native origins follows. Along with the Fourth of July, Thanksgiving has become a favorite time for the mass media to observe general American society's adaptation of Native American ideas as well as material artifacts in recent years.

1989.018. Brown, Bruce. "A Native American Sampler." *Washington Post Book World*, May 17, 1989, p. 6.

A review of four books, one of them Weatherford's *Indian Givers*, cites *Forgotten Founders* as a source for Weatherford's argument on political influence.

1989. 019. Cox, Patrick. "Banning Peyote Use Would Be Injustice." *USA Today*, November 10, 1989, p. 14-A.

In light of laws that ban use of drugs (such as peyote) in Native American religious rituals, Cox asserts that "It is ironic that the Articles of Confederation, the foundation of our Constitution, was based explicitly on the rules of the Iroquois Confederation. It is more ironic that so few people know it." This is one of a number of instances in which Native Americans' ability to provide intellectual inspiration to American society is used to illustrate that Native American religious practices also have value and should be protected by law.

1989.020. Drummond, Tammerlin. "Inauguration is Time of Opportunity...Native American Writes Poetically of U.S. Emblem." St. Petersburg *Times*, January 20, 1989, p. 1.

This is an interview with Gabriel Horn, co-author of a new book, *The American Eagle*, which was being considered by the Bush administration as a "gift of state," to be presented to visiting dignitaries. Horn, who writes under the name White Deer of Autumn (which his parents gave him at birth), says of the American Eagle: "Few people know that the Eagle Symbol of the United States of America...was originally the symbol of the Ho-de-no-saunee, or Iroquois....[The United States] also borrowed ideas of democracy from the People of the Longhouse."

1989.021. Flynn, Johnny P. "Pass the Turkey...and the Medicine, the Laws..." Los Angeles *Times* [op-ed pages], November 23, 1989, p. B-11.

Flynn, a doctoral candidate in Native American religions at the University of California/Santa Barbara, gives a Thanksgiving outline of Indian contributions to general American life. "Both the French and American revolutions were advanced, in part, because colonists had seen, in Indian forms of government, how the democratic structure functioned when people elected leaders who debated issues in public forums. But scholars here and abroad still resist the conclusion that the Iroquois Great Law of Peace somehow contributed to the U.S. Constitution, the Bill of Rights, the bicameral legislature and the separation of powers." Flynn adds, however, that "Frederich Engels wrote in 1879 that the *Communist Manifesto* 'would have been far different' had he and Karl Marx known what they later learned about Indian forms of government."

1989.022. Goodman, Howard, "An Age-old Ceremony of Peace for the Planet." Philadelphia *Inquirer*, May 2, 1989, pp. B-1, B-2.

Report on a conference entitled "Forgotten Legacy: Native American Concepts and the Formation of United States Government," organized in Philadelphia by Toni Truesdale, the United Indians of the Delaware Valley, *et al.* Files contain a program of the conference. Grinde and Johansen appeared on a panel at this conference, which Tooker attended. The debate which ensued is described in Johansen and Grinde, "Recent Historiography," [1990]. Goodman attended the planting of a white pine in a Philadelphia park, but missed the debate that Grinde and Johansen had with Tooker later in the conference. The reporter bought a copy of *Forgotten Founders* from Johansen, but still called him "Johnson" in the article.

1989.023. Grenard, Steve. "Surprise! We Got Our Constitution From An Indian Tribe." *National Enquirer*, January 17, 1989, p. 36.

The largest popular audience for the "influence thesis" to date was provided by one of the less-raunchy tabloid weeklies. Surprisingly, considering the source (and its editors' overstated headline), the factual material in this article is generally accurate, even though Grenard's analysis is exaggerated in typical *Enquirer* style.

1989.024. Hall, C. Ray. "Q and A Test, U.S. Constitution." Louisville *Courier-Journal*, September 17, 1989, p. 10-M[Magazine].

This long (4,975-word) piece on constitutional trivia observes that John Rutledge based the preamble of the document ("We the People...) on phrasing that had come to him from the Iroquois.

1989.025. Hilderbrand, John. "Anti-minority Bias Seen in State Education Guides." *Newsday*, July 29, 1989, p. 7.

This is a report on the release of "A Curriculum of Inclusion" by New York State education officials. "The report also concluded that minorities' cultural contributions had been consistently downgraded. It cited the failure of history textbooks to describe the role of black soldiers who fought on both sides in the American Revolution. Also mentioned was the scant attention paid to the Iroquois Indians, whose system of government was said to have contributed significantly to New York State's constitution." [Perhaps he means "U.S. Constitution."]

1989.026. Johansen, Bruce. "Indian Culture Played Part in Founding of Democracy." Omaha *World-Herald*, Dec. 31, 1989, p. 21-A.

This op-ed column is a reply to George Will's first swipe at the New York Curriculum of Inclusion, from which his 1991 column [see Johansen, 1991 and Will, 1991] may have been borrowed. "In his rush to embrace European culture, Will forgets that the founders of the United States didn't go to all the trouble of rebelling against England solely to replicate European models here." The text of the column was synthesized from an early draft of *Exemplar of Liberty* [1991].

1989.027. Mathewson, Judy. [Untitled; dispatch of States News Service] October 3, 1989.

Anthony Lee, a senior at George W. Fowler High School, testified before the U.S. House of Representatives Select Committee on Children, Youth, and Families and the Budget Committee Task Force on Human Resources. Lee, son of a Mohawk father, told the members of the two committees: "Do you know that Native Americans have played a major role in forming our present government? Did you know that the government succeeded in forming our Constitution by replicating the Iroquois Confederacy? You probably have never heard of these facts, and this is why I strongly believe that more Native American history should be taught." This hearing was convened to call attention to the first National Children's Day on October 8, 1989.

1989.028. Reid, T.R. "A Century After the Indian Wars, Clash Over Sovereignty Persists." Washington *Post*, March 5, 1989, p. A-1.

Reporting from Rocky Boy, Montana, Reid describes how a U.S. official was charged by the Chippewa-Cree after he had impounded their horses, a test of sovereignty. Reid reflects on Indian political systems more generally, as well, observing that "Benjamin Franklin later observed that the Iroquois Confederacy influenced Madison's design for federalism." The example is being used here to illustrate that Native American concepts of sovereignty are being actively exercised in the contemporary world.

1989.029. Weatherford, Jack. "Indians and the 4th [of July]." Baltimore *Evening Sun*, July 3, 1989.

This opinion column summarizes the impact of native thought and practice on American political ideas, from *Indian Givers*, a book that surveys both material and intellectual contributions of American Indians to general North American society.

1989.030. Weiner, Mark. "Onondagas Again Hold Wampum Belts." Sunday [Syracuse] *Herald-American* and *Post-Standard*, October 22, 1989, p. A-1.

This report on the return of wampum belts to the Iroquois by the State of New York quotes Oren Lyons: "You're looking at the democratic foundation of perhaps the world." Later in the article, author Mark Weiner states that the Hiawatha Belt can be traced to the origins of the Iroquois Confederacy, whose great law is considered by many to have directly influenced the U.S. Constitution." John Fadden reports that Gail Schaeefer, New York Secretary of State, raised the issue of Iroquois influence on democracy in her speech at this event.

1988

Books, Scholarly and Specialty Journals

1988.001. Allen, Paula Gunn. "Who is Your Mother? Red Roots of White Feminism." in Rick Simonson and Scott Walker, *The Graywolf Annual Five: Multicultural Literacy*. St. Paul: Graywolf Press, 1988, pp. 13-27.

In work that is in some ways similar to that of Sally Roesch Wagner, Paula Gunn Allen traces native influences on the evolution of feminist thought. "The root of oppression is the loss of memory" (p. 18), Allen writes, particularly, in this case, when the lost memory involves the influence of the Native American intellect in history. "Neither Greece nor Rome had the kind of pluralistic democracy as that concept has been understood in the United States since Andrew Jackson, but the tribes, especially the gynarchial tribal confederacies, did." (p. 23)

1988.002. Axtell, James. *After Columbus: Essays in the Ethnohistory of Colonial North America*. New York: Oxford University Press, 1988.

Page 252: Indians invented scalping, but democracy -- no way! "Another myth, which floated up once again at Kahnawake and is very much before us during the bicentennial, is that the United States Constitution was closely patterned upon the League of the Iroquois. Each myth [this one, and the purported European invention of scalping] contains just enough truth to be plausible, but they are logically and historically fallacious. Should the scholar risk the displeasure of the disabused by constantly and forcefully saying so?" To empower his logic, and his ability to discern historical validity, Axtell footnotes this assertion with two of his own works, an article in the New York *Times* [see 1987], Tooker's "U.S. Constitution and the Iroquois League" in draft, and an M.A. thesis by a student at William and Mary, [Nancy Dieter Egloff, "'Six Nations of Ignorant Savages:' Benjamin Franklin and the Iroquois League of Nations." M.A. thesis, College of William and Mary, 1987].

1988.003. Barreiro, Jose, ed. *Indian Roots of American Democracy*. Ithaca, N.Y.: Cornell American Indian Program, 1988.

Printed proceedings of the September, 1987 conference "Cultural Encounter: The Iroquois Great Law of Peace and the United States Constitution." The conference, the first on the subject, brought together traditional Iroquois, scholars, and others to examine the Great Law, its history, and its impact on subsequent political events.

1988.004. Barreiro, Jose. "Commentary." *Northeast Indian Quarterly*, Fall, 1988, pp. 4, 52.

Barreiro, editor of *NEIQ*, describes opposition to the *Haudenosaunee* curriculum, then surveys the debate over the "influence thesis," giving it that name for the first time. Summarizing the results of the 1987 Cornell conference on the subject, Barreiro compares the controversy to that aroused by Martin Bernal's *Black Athena*. He concludes: "It would be most valuable now to have proponents and opponents of the influence thesis present their conclusions at a public forum." (p. 52)

1988.005. Burton, Bruce A. "A Call to Classroom Consciousness: Reflections on Teaching American History." *Turtle Quarterly* Winter, 1988, pp. 6-10.

Advocates revision of school curricula to include the "influence thesis."

1988.006. Fresia, Jerry. *Toward an American Revolution: Exposing the Constitution and Other Illusions*. Boston: South End Press, 1988.

Fresia brings the Iroquois Great Law of Peace into his discussion of the U.S. Constitution's ideological shortcomings. On pages 75 and 76, he writes: "For the Iroquois, the concept of 'the people' meant something very different from what the Framers had in mind. Their law and custom provided for the relatively equitable distribution of wealth, universal suffrage, and a confederation of states similar to the one described in the Articles [of Confederation]." Fresia quotes Cadwallader Colden (in 1727) on Iroquois notions of liberty, treatment of leaders as servants of the people, etc., referencing *Forgotten Founders* [1982, 1987].

1988.007. Johansen, Bruce. "Vox Americana." *Northeast Indian Quarterly*, Fall, 1988, pp. 18-25.

This is a survey of Native American confederate models in eastern North America, as well as early European-Americans' descriptions of them, with an emphasis how the European observers related them to their ideas of liberty. It is from an early draft of *Exemplar of Liberty* [1991], chapter of the same name.

1988.008. Johansen. "Democracy and a Constitution: Indian Influences on the United States." *Turtle Quarterly*, Winter, 1988, pp. 2-5.

Survey of the Indian image in revolutionary American thought, describing events between Cannassatego's 1744 speech at Lancaster, through the Albany Plan (1754) and the years of the revolution.

1988.009. Smith, Lisa M. "Working Pictures Signs Blume..." *Back Stage*, February 5, 1988.

This article says that the film company Working Pictures is planning to "draw the board and shoot the series of four public-service announcements exploring the origins of the Constitution and its roots in the Iroquois Confederacy."

1988.010. Tooker, Elisabeth. "The United States Constitution and the Iroquois League." *Ethnohistory* 35:4(Fall, 1988), pp. 305-336.

This was the first detailed rebuttal in a scholarly journal in reaction to assertion of the "influence thesis" during the 1980s. Tooker reviews some of the evidence advanced to support the thesis, but alleges that proponents believe that the Founders "copied" the Constitution from the Iroquois League. This is obviously not the case, Tooker finds, because U.S. government is based on majority rule, not unanimous consensus, and U.S. senators are not nominated by their clan mothers. Tooker believes that the Founders were almost entirely ignorant of Iroquois and other native political systems. "Not until Lewis H. Morgan made it a special subject of study and published his findings did an account of the Iroquois form of government become available." (p. 311) Tooker does quote a passage in Morgan's *Houses and House-life of the American Aborigines* (1881) in which the founder of American anthropology says that the Iroquois "commended to our forefathers a union of colonies as early as 1755." (p. 324), but she seems historically oblivious to the copious (but not "systematic") observations of Jefferson, Franklin, Paine, Adams, and others during the founding of the United States. The "influence thesis" is "a myth," according to Tooker. (p. 321), started by a press release issued on Smithsonian letterhead on March 26, 1936 by ethnologist J.N.B. Hewitt. In footnote 2 (p. 330), Tooker reveals that while she "relied heavily" on *Forgotten Founders* for her list of statements attributing political influence to the Iroquois, "I attempt here no consideration of all the questionable interpretations of the data such authors as Johansen and Grinde make...."

1988.011. Wagner, Sally Roesch. "The Iroquois Confederacy: A Native American Model for Non-sexist Men." *Changing Men*, Spring-summer, 1988, p. 32-33.

This article is a concise survey of Iroquois governance from a feminist perspective, as a model for present-day gender relations. Wagner, who had spent most of two decades studying the nineteenth century roots of feminism, was discovering in the late 1980s that a century and more earlier Matilda Joslyn Gage and Elizabeth Cady Stanton had associated with the Iroquois and used their society as an example of gender relations that was more equitable than the nineteenth-century United States, where a wife was regarded as her husband's property. Wagner developed this theme in several later articles, and during the 1990s was working on a book-length history of feminism's Native American roots.

1988.012. Weatherford, Jack. *Indian Givers: How the Indians of the Americas Transformed the World.* New York: Crown, 1988.

Three chapters of this trade book delve into Native American political practices; two of them quote liberally (with citations) from *Forgotten Founders* [1982, 1987]. Johansen and Weatherford began corresponding and exchanging manuscripts in 1988; Johansen edited an early draft of his sequel *Native Roots*. Johansen also supplied Weatherford with an early draft of *Exemplar of Liberty* [1991], which is cited as a reference in *Native Roots*. During the next decade, Weatherford's *Indian Givers* became one of the most widely cited sources in support of assertions that the Iroquois helped shape democracy.

Newspapers and Magazines

1988.013. _____. "Northeast Wisconsin News Briefs." [United Press International] May 19, 1988.

In Oneida, Wisconsin, the Oneida Tribe of Indians will observe the bicentennial of the signing of the United States Constitution to call attention to contributions of Native Americans toward the writing of the document. The tribe will hold a Great Tree of Peace ceremony at the Norbert Hill Center in Oneida.

1988.014. _____. "Philippine Minister Challenges North on Democracy." [Interpress Service] May 5, 1988.

Raul Manglapus, Philippine Foreign Secretary, is challenging the industrial world's assumptions about its primacy in the theory of democracy at a ministerial meeting of the 21-nation Council of Europe at its headquarters in Strasborg, Germany. "The democratic value that is the heart of the constitution of the Council of Europe is indigenous not only to the northern societies, but to all human cultures..." Manglapus said, according to this account, "citing democratic republics like Licchavis, developed on the Indian subcontinent 600 years before Christ, [and] the Iroquois Confederacy that preceded the United States Constitution..."

1988.015. _____. "Pow Wow Opens in Baltimore." [United Press International], August 26, 1988.

More than 29,000 people are expected in Baltimore today for one of the largest pow-wows on the East Coast. Barry Richardson, chairman of the pow-wow committee, "said American Indians also celebrate the formation of the U.S. Constitution, which, he said, contains Indian principles such as initiative, recall, referendum, and equal suffrage."

1988.016. Banks, Gail. "Indian Givers." *Boston Magazine,* November, 1988, pp. 140, 143-145.

Review of four books on Native American topics, two of which are *Forgotten Founders* [1987] and Paula Gunn Allen's *The Sacred Hoop* [1988].

1988.017. Barreiro, Jose. "The Iroquois Influence: Cornell Conference Showed Ties to U.S. Constitution, Syracuse *Post-Standard*, Oct. 12, 1988, p. A-11.

This op-ed piece is similar in some ways to Barreiro's "Commentary," above, tailored as a response to James Axtell's comments in Farrell, below.

1988.018. Binder, David and Martin Tolchin. "Washington Talk, Briefing: The First Constitution." New York *Times*, September 12, 1988.

Announcement of an Iroquois gathering at Constitution Park to plant a white pine and observe, as the authors put it, that "the Iroquois constitution [was] woven into the United States Constitution."

1988.019. Boslet, Mark. "Contributions of Indians Told at Columbus Day Event." Waterbury *Republican* [Waterbury, Conn.] October 11, 1988, pp. B-1, B-2.

Bruce Burton, English professor at Castleton State College, Vermont, describes Native American contributions to the trans-Atlantic flow of ideas.

1988.020. Dougherty, Philip H. "American Indian Group Sponsors Ad Campaign." New York *Times*, July 27, 1988, p. D-18 [Financial desk].

"Although it is still considered a controversial theory in educational circles, the idea that our Founding Fathers were inspired in creating our Constitution by the ancient Iroquois Confederacy is presented as fact in a new public-service advertising campaign...."

1988.021. Farrell, Marybeth. [Untitled; Dispatch from States News Service] October 4, 1988.

New York State education officials say that passage of a resolution citing the Iroquois Confederacy's contributions to democracy by the U.S. House of Representatives will not impact the rewriting of the state's curriculum for history. P. Alistair MacKinnon, the New York State Education Department's co-ordinator of federal education, said the resolution, which has no legal force, "would not sway the department's assessment of whether the confederacy's constitution...was the model for the U.S. Constitution, as some members of the Confederacy have said."

1988.022. Farrell, Marybeth. [Untitled; dispatch from States News Service] September 30, 1988.

This account details views related to a resolution observing Iroquois contributions to American democracy in the U.S. Senate. The effort is said to be spearheaded by Oren Lyons with the help of Senators Daniel Inouye and Daniel Evans, who are chair and vice-chair respectively of the Senate Select Committee on Indian Affairs. Francis Jennings, director emeritus of the D'Arcy McNickle Center for the History of the American Indian, says that the resolution "destroys my faith in the historical literacy of the Senate." The article quotes Donald Grinde in support of "influence," and a number of historians against the idea.

1988.023. Farrell, Marybeth. [States News Service], October 26, 1988.

Datelined Washington,D.C., this news article says that Gerald F. Heath, an owner of New Day Productions (a film company) is trying to get President Reagan to endorse a project "to teach students of all ages about the Iroquois Confederacy of Nation's [*sic*] influence on the U.S. Constitution." [Files contain a letter to this effect; Johansen's personal files contain copious correspondence with a half-dozen other film makers who have expressed an interest in the the idea since 1985.] The article also refers to the resolutions supporting this idea passed by the U.S. Senate and House.

1988.024. Farrell, Marybeth. "Historians Debunk Iroquois Influence on the Constitution," States News Service in Syracuse *Post-Standard*, September 24, 1988, p. A-3.

"They just swallowed a public-relations effort by one small faction of the Iroquois folks," says James Axtell, Kenan Professor of Humanities at the College of William and Mary [and incoming president of the American Society for Ethnohistory] of a resolution passed by the U.S. Senate attributing the origins of American political thought in part to the Iroquois Confederacy. The article also quotes Ben Nighthorse Campbell, representative from Colorado, in support of the influence idea, which is expressed in a resolution he is sponsoring in the House of Representatives.   [Campbell was elected to the U.S. Senate from Colorado in 1992.]

1988.025. Farrell, Marybeth. [States News Service] September 17, 1988.

Report on the tree-planting at the National Mall in Washington, D.C. that ignited Michael Newman's condescension in *The New Republic.* [below]. This article is more balanced than Newman's, quoting Oren Lyons, Onondaga faithkeeper, and Grinde in support of the "influence thesis," and Walter F. Berns, Georgetown University professor and author, against.

1988.026. Grinde, Donald A., Jr. [Letter to the editor], Washington *Post,* April 30, 1988.

Reply regarding Charles Krauthammer's piece [below] "bemoaning the fact that Stanford emasculated its core curriculum in Western civilization...[in favor of]...'cultural diversity....'" Grinde cites the debt of American government to Iroquois precedents.

1988.027. Johansen, Bruce. "President's Remarks Showed Ignorance of the Past." Alliance [Nebraska] *Times-Herald,* June 20, 1988.

In this reprint of an Omaha *World-Herald* op-ed piece, Johansen takes issue with remarks on American Indians made by President Ronald Reagan at Moscow University. Reagan had said that the United States "humored" Indians with treaties and reservations. The article asserts that Indian influences are woven into the United States national character, and that Reagan is ignorant of most of them. The original op-ed piece was published by the Omaha *World-Herald* June 16, 1988, p. 19.

1988.028. Kahn, Daniel. "Agency Takes Up Challenge for Free." *Newsday,* August 1, 1988, p. 5.

In this business-section story, Kahn describes the efforts Drossman, Lehmann Marino, a New York City advertising agency, on behalf of Amerinda, a Native American advocacy group. These efforts include creation of a print advertisement and poster that show an Iroquois wampum belt over the headline "You're Looking at the First Draft of the Constitution." The agency also is said to have produced a public-service video spot on the same theme. The story noted that the agency, which usually accepts only multi-million dollar accounts from corporate clients, created this public-service campaign on a budget of $10,000.

1988.029. Krauthammer, Charles. "A Battle Lost at Stanford." Washington *Post*, April 22, 1988.

Bill King, a student leader of a protest at Stanford, is reported by Krauthammer to have said, among other things, that established college curricula ignore the fact that "the Iroquois Indians in America had a representative democracy which served as a model for the American system." Krauthammer is making a case against reforms in curricula such as those adopted in the late 1980s at Stanford.

1988.030. Newman, Michael. "The Iroquois and the Constitution: Founding Feathers." *New Republic*, November 7, 1988, pp. 17-18.

Newman ridicules a gathering of American Indians to plant a symbolic Iroquois tree of peace on the National Mall in Washington, D.C., calling their ceremonies "hokey" and assertions of Indian influence on the Constitution a "myth [that] isn't just silly. It's destructive." Newman then lectures American Indians, asserting that they should shelve philosophical debates and concentrate on their present-day economic problems. [Files contain unpublished letters from Grinde and Johansen (and one signed by both) to Newman and the editors of the *New Republic*.]

1988.031. Peck, Ira. "The People of the Longhouse." *Junior Scholastic*, October 21, 1988, pp. 12-14.

Briefly describes Iroquois governance, and its effect on the colonists, especially Benjamin Franklin.

1988.032. Tewkesbury, Don. "NW[Northwest] Tribes Angry at Reagan's Remark." Seattle *Post-Intelligencer*, June 1, 1988, p. A-9.

Joe de la Cruz, president of the Quinault Nation Council, says that when President Reagan told students at Moscow University that the United States "humored" American Indians by providing reservations for them, he was ignoring the debt that U. S. institutions owe native precedents. "The president is like a lot of Americans who do not understand the United States' own Constitution and the reason for the treaties, which are part of the law of the land. That is because American history does not teach the part that the Indians played in the formation of the U.S. Constitution."

1988.033. Venables, Robert W. "Reagan Remarks Insult Native Americans." [Letter to the editor] New York *Times*, June 23, 1988, p. A-22.

Venables, a visiting associate professor in Cornell University's American Indian Program, rebuts assertions by President Ronald Reagan at Moscow University that the United States "humored" "primitive" Indians by establishing reservations. "As a label derogating an entire race," writes Venables, "'primitive' could hardly be applied to the Mayas of Mesoamerica, the builders of the Chaco Canyon complex in New Mexico, or the political democracy of the Iroquois in the Northeast, who recognized women's political and economic rights centuries before Europe and the United States."

1987

Books, Scholarly and Specialty Journals

1987.001. _____. "From One Sovereign People to Another," *National Geographic*, September, 1987, pp. 370-373.

This article briefly describes the Iroquois Great Law of Peace, then asks: "Could it be that the U.S. Constitution owes a debt to the Iroquois?" The article describes Franklin's view of native politics.

1987.002. _____. "Selected Readings on Iroquois Contributions to the U. S. Constitution." *Northeast Indian Quarterly* 4:3 (Fall, 1987), p. 29.

This was probably the first attempt at a bibliography for the "influence" issue. Significantly, it was carried in Jose Barreiro's *Northeast Indian Quarterly*, which helped sponsor the Cornell American Indian Program conference on the subject in 1987.

1987.003. Johansen, Bruce E. *Forgotten Founders: How the American Indian Helped Shape Democracy*. Boston: Harvard Common Press/Gambit, 1987.

Paperback edition of *Forgotten Founders: Benjamin Franklin, the Iroquois and the Rationale for the American Revolution*, published in 1982 by Gambit, Inc., of Ipswich, Mass. [Reviews of this edition appeared in the Philadelphia *Inquirer* (October 4, 1987), The Milwaukee *Journal* (Sept. 22, 1987) the Cleveland *Plain Dealer* (December 6, 1987), and *The Bloomsbury Review* "The Best of 1987," November/December, 1987.]

1987.004. Johansen. "Philosopher as Savage: Benjamin Franklin and the Iroquois." *Northeast Indian Quarterly* 4:3 (Fall, 1987), pp. 21-28.

Excerpt from *Forgotten Founders.*

1987.005. Kickingbird, Kirke, and Lynn Shelby Kickingbird. *Indians and the United States Constitution: A Forgotten Legacy*. Oklahoma City and Washington, D.C.: Institute for the Development of Indian Law, 1987.

This 36-page booklet provides an overview of Native American contributions to American political thought. It cites from several primary sources, and *Forgotten Founders* [1982, 1987]. The Kickingbirds' was the first of several explorations of the "influence" idea in legal forums and journals.

1987.006. Mee, Charles L., Jr. *The Genius of the People*. New York: Harper & Row, 1987.

On page 237, at the beginning of the chapter titled "Details," Mee notes that the Committee of Detail (on the U.S. Constitution) met daily. "[John] Rutledge [chairman of the committee] always admired the Iroquois Indians, particularly their legal system, which gave autonomy for their internal affairs, but united them for purposes of war." Mee says that Rutledge opened a meeting of the Committee of Detail by reading from an Iroquois treaty dated 1520, which began "We, the people, to form a union, to establish peace, equity, and order..." Concludes Mee: "He commended he phrasings to his colleagues -- and so, in some part, the preamble to the new constitution was based on the law of the land as it had been on the east coast before the first white settlers arrived." Mee's thumbnail description of Rutledge has had a long life; as this bibliography went to press, it was cited in a discussion on the Internet that began in Quebec, shortly after an independence referendum narrowly failed there in the fall of 1995.

1987.007. Tokar, Brian. *The Green Alternative: Creating an Ecological Future.* San Pedro, California: R. E. Miles, 1987.

On page 13, Tokar writes that "Probably the most influential model of democracy in this hemisphere was the Iroquois Confederacy..." as he quotes the Mohawk Nation's Basic Call to Consciousness (1978) on how "the Haudenosaunee became the first 'United Nations.'" On the next page, however, Tokar writes: "Obviously, we cannot simply 'go back' to a tribal way of life....Tribal cultures are not an ideal to which we should want to return. They are not models for us to copy." Tokar says that "primitive cultures were sometimes very warlike," and that their democracies broke down in times of war. Tokar does not hold old-world societies to the same standards that he does Native American confederacies. The Greeks, for example, had a hard time maintaining their vestiges of democracy in the face of war as well.

1987.008. Ywahoo, Dhyani. *Voices of Our Ancestors: Cherokee Teachings From the Wisdom Fire.* Boston: Shambhala, 1987.

This new-age treatment briefly mentions Native American governance and its influence on that of the United States on pages 16 and 144, with no references. This is one of a number of enthusiastic treatments of the "influence" issue by "new age" authors, some of whom have been accused of being "plastic medicine men" by Native American traditionalists.

Newspapers, Newsletters, and Magazines

1987.009. _____. "Celebration Planned Here for Constitution's Bicentennial." *Cornell Chronicle* 19:3 (September 10, 1987), pp. 1,7.

The newspaper of Cornell's administration featured side-by-side announcements of two conferences scheduled during September at the university: the American Indian Program's conference on the Great Law of Peace and the Constitution (Sept. 11-12), and another conference a week later that featured a speech by former senator and secretary of state Edmund S. Muskie. The AIP conference drew 400 people, while the "mainstream" conference registered about 100.

1987.010. _____. "Iroquois Constitution: A Forerunner to Colonists['] Democratic Principles." New York *Times*, June 28, 1987, p. 40.

Quotes Oren Lyons in support of the "influence thesis;" revision of New York State school curricula to include the idea also is mentioned.

1987.011. _____. "Iroquois Great Law and Constitution Conference Set." *IPN Weekly Report* 3:35 (August 31, 1987).

1987.012. _____. "With All Due Respect to the 'Founding Fathers:' Indian Contributions to the U.S. Constitution." Friends Committee on National Legislation, Washington, D.C., August-September, 1987.

The first four pages of this eight-page newsletter outline Native American contributions to the ideological corpus of U.S. democracy, highlighting the role of the Iroquois and Benjamin Franklin.

1987.013. _____. "Experts Discuss Indian Influence on U.S. Constitution." [United Press International] September 11, 1987.

This is a brief announcement of the September, 1987, conference at Cornell University the following week to discuss the relationship of the Iroquois confederate structure and the evolution of American democracy.

1987.014. _____. "The Iroquois and the Constitution." The Washington *Post*, August 25, 1987, p. B-5.

Brief announcement of a speech by Oren Lyons, September 3 at the University of Virginia, as part of a program marking the Constitution's bicentennial. Lyons will speak on "The Origins of the Democratic Principles of Governance." The news items notes that Lyons "has focussed his research on documenting the Iroquois influence on the Constitution."

1987.015. _____. "Arts Scene." *Christian Science Monitor*, August 20, 1987, p. 22.

"A free show in New York's Prospect Park is planned September 12, when Bread and Puppet Theater performs an outdoor spectacle with the U.S. Constitution and an Iroquois Indian document as its theme."

1987.016. Andrews, Dan. "City Officials Pay Tribute to 'The Great Experiment.'" [United Press International] September 17, 1987.

A gathering of New York City officials and their guests paid tribute to the signing of the Constitution 200 years ago. "...A hushed audience listened as Chief Leon Shenandoah told them the history of the Six Nations Iroquois Confederacy, whose unwritten 'constitution' served as a guide for the framers of the Constitution."

1987.017. Debevec, Charles E. "Minnesota Issues." [United Press International] May 23, 1987.

Kirke Kickingbird will speak in St. Paul, Minn. June 10 "about the influence of the Iroquois Indian Federation on the drafters of the Constitution."

1987.018. Denvir, John. "A Book for the Bork Debate." [Review of Mee, *Genius of the People*] Los Angeles *Times*, September 20, 1987, p. 16[Book Review].

Denvir, who teaches constitutional law at the University of San Francisco Law School, says, with Mee, that "The majestic 'We the people' which opens the Constitution was most likely copied from an Iroquois document."

1987.019. Faber, Harold. "Indian History Alive at New York Site." New York *Times*, July 26, 1987, Section 1, p. 36.

Ganondagan, in Central New York State, is dedicated as the state's first Native American State Historic Site. As part of his article, Faber quotes Seneca scholar John Mohawk, who created the texts for 70 stainless-steel signs at the historic site: "The Six Nation Confederacy played a pivotal role not only in Indian affairs but in the thinking of men like Benjamin Franklin and Thomas Jefferson when it came to drafting plans for how the United States was to be governed. And so their legacy had some effect on the Declaration of Independence, the Constitution, and the Bill of Rights, with which we live today."

1987.020. Fadden, Steven. "Forgotten Founders of the Constitution." *The Grapevine* (Ithaca, NY), September 10-16, 1987, p. 7.

Description of program to be held Sept. 11-12 at Cornell University, with detail on speakers.

1987.021. Ferziger, Jonathan. "Special Constitution Package..." [United Press International] August 25, 1987.

This is a review of the events attending the ratification of the U.S. Constitution in New York State and its celebration two hundred years later. Ferziger reports that the state bicentennial commission also developed a series of "Constitutional Minutes" for television, including one on "the state's first great constitution-maker, the legendary Hiawatha, who brought New York's Indian tribes together in the Iroquois Confederation even before the white man discovered the continent."

1987.022. Fiske, Edward B. "New York Revamps Social Studies." New York *Times*, October 20, 1987, p. B-1.

New York is one of two influential states (the other is California) to release new curriculum guidelines this year. In New York, "for the first time, 7th and 11th grade American history guidelines include a discussion of a controversial theory that the Iroquois Confederacy, a coalition of tribes, had considerable influence on the framers of the United States Constitution."

1987.023. Glover, J. Denis. [of *The Christian Science Monitor*], "Forebears of the Founding Fathers. Los Angeles *Times*, December 11, 1987, part 8, page 5.

This piece, datelined Concord, Mass., quotes Slow Turtle on "the Iroquois League, and Indian ideas of confederation as a foundation for the Constitution. He asserts that John Rutledge borrowed the preamble of the Constitution ["We the people...") from the Iroquois. His companion, Medicine Story, says that the founders studied the Iroquois government.

1987.024. Johansen, Bruce. "The Oldest Constitution?" [Letter to the editor] *American Heritage*, September/October 1987, p. 14.

The magazine's special edition on the U.S. Constitution is said to have missed contributions by Native Americans, particularly the Iroquois. Johansen briefly outlines Native American contributions to democracy and Native American symbols in revolutionary-era artwork.

1987.025. Johnson, Tim. "Indians Trace Roots of Constitution." *Daybreak* 1:1 (Autumn, 1987), pp. 3-5.

1987.026. Mohawk, John. "We, the Original People: A Celebration of the Principles of Democracy." *Daybreak* 1:1 (Autumn, 1987), pp. 2, 6-9.

1987.027. Myers, Mike. "Those Ill-served." [Letter to the editor] *Time*, July 27, 1987, p. 6.

Myers, a Seneca who is executive director of Native Futures on the Onondaga Nation, writes "to comment on [*Time's*] presentation of Native Americans." Myers says that the Iroquois Confederacy is among the world's oldest continuously functioning democracies...[which] provided a model for political organization that endures to this day."

1987.028. Naedele, Walter F. "An American Constitution Much Older Than 200 Years." Philadelphia *Inquirer*, May 7, 1987.

John Kahionhes Fadden, Mohawk artist and teacher, supports the idea that the Iroquois helped shape American political institutions. The article mentions Franklin's relationship with the Iroquois, his comments on their government, and Cannassatego's 1744 speech at Lancaster.

1987.029. Prince, Richard. "Constitution Owes Much to 'Indian Givers.'" Rochester [New York] *Democrat and Chronicle*, May 21, 1987.

This editorial column outlines Iroquois governance and Franklin's comments on it, citing from *Forgotten Founders*.

1987.030. St. John, Jeffrey. "Constitutional Journal." *Christian Science Monitor*, July 27, 1987, p. 32.

This piece, the 46th in a series on the ratification of the U.S. Constitution, says that Charles Rutledge adopted the "We the People" phrasing of the preamble "from a constitution drawn up in 1520 by five Iroquois Indian nations."

1987.031. St. John, Jeffrey. "Constitutional Journal." *Christian Science Monitor*, July 24. 1987, p. 28.

In part 45 of a continuing series on the formulation of the Constitution, "John Rutledge is reported to have opened today's session by pulling from his pocket a copy of a constitution drawn up in 1520 by five Iroquois Indian nations." According to this account, Rutledge then recited from the document for the four other members of the Committee of Detail: "We, the people, to form a union, to establish peace, equity, and order..." The use of the term "a copy" is curious here, since significant portions of the Iroquois Great Law of Peace were not committed to European-style writing until the late nineteenth century. A truly comprehensive version was not published in English until 1992. Suffice to say that Rutledge utilized Iroquois example, but not as graphically as this article has it.

1987.032. Shatz, Frank. "Iroquois Affected the Constitution." *The Virginia Gazette,* Sept. 19, 1987, n.p.

This "World Focus" column in a newspaper serving Williamsburg, York, and James City, Virginia says "There is growing recognition that the American colonists' association with Native American Indians had a profound influence on the framers of the U.S. Constitution." The article quotes John Kahionhes Fadden, and describes Iroquois notions of freedom and federalism, as well as early interactions between colonists, notably Benjamin Franklin, and native peoples.

1987.033. Shogren, Elizabeth. [United Press International] August 20, 1987.

Shogren quotes Oren Lyons on Iroquois history and the Great Law's relationship to U.S. fundamental law. Also quotes Johansen in support of the "influence thesis," with Michael Kammen, Cornell professor of history in opposition, saying that "There is no scholarly evidence to support the claims of the Iroquois Confederacy on the Founders."

1987.034. Stanich, Susan. "Iroquois Roots Grow Deep in the U.S. Constitution." Seattle *Times,* October 11, 1987, p. A-16.

1987.035. Yarrow, Andrew L. "Weekender Guide." New York *Times,* September 11, 1987, p. C-1.

At Prospect Park in Brooklyn, oversized puppets and paper-mache animals are part of the cast of the Bread and Puppet Theater as it performs "The Archetypal Slogan Circus." The writer describes the "Circus" as "part allegory and part comedy...includ[ing] puppets representing the Founding Fathers as well as women and landless Americans who were neglected by the Constitution. The 90-minute show was inspired not only by the Constitution, but also by its Iroquois precursor, known as 'Kaianerekowa' [The Great Binding Law or Great Law of Peace]."

Congressional Resolution

1987.036. [December 2] Hearing, U.S. Senate Select Committee on Indian Affairs, on S. Con. Res. 76, "To acknowledge the contribution of the Iroquois Confederacy of Nations to the development of the United States Constitution..." The hearing was held in Washington, D.C. A transcript is available.

1975 - 1986

Books, Scholarly and Specialty Journals

1975.001. _____. "Iroquois Irony." *Akwesasne Notes*, Early Summer, 1981, p. 28.

In Montreal, during a meeting between Native Americans and Marxists, one of the non-Indian Marxists asked Mohawk Nation Council subchief Tom Porter to stop emphasizing religious matters. Porter then told the Marxist of the Iroquois Great Law and its influence on the United States' founders, as well as Marx and Engels. "Therefore, sire, you understand that it's not Marx's great-grandson who will come and dictate the way to manage our business," Porter is reported to have said. [Reprinted from *The Atlantean Era*, Feb. 27, 1980.]

1975.002. Austin, Alberta. *"Ne'Ho Niyo' De:No': That's What it Was Like.* Lackawanna, N.Y.: Rebco Enterprises, 1986.

This is one of two volumes compiled by the Seneca Nation Curriculum Development Project during the 1980s, which records the memories of Iroquois elders. Most are Seneca, but all the other nations are represented. One of the accounts (pp. 174-183) is from Leon Shenondoah (or Shenandoah; spellings vary), Tadadaho (speaker) of the Haudenosaunee central council at Onondaga. On the subject of constitutional influence (pp. 177-178), he says: "When the United States copied our form of government in the 1750s, they left out spirituality. This is what I learned as a child....Our religion is within the government and our government is within our religion. It is entwined. If the government goes off to one side...the religion will then pull you back in line...[One] counteracts the other....But when the United States joined the 13 colonies and copied our form of government, they held their meetings in one house, and their church (their beliefs) in another house....It's not under the same roof like we do."

1975.003. Bagley, Carol and Jo Ann Ruckman, "Iroquois Contributions to Modern Democracy and Communism." *American Indian Culture & Research Journal*, 7:2(1983), pp. 53-72.

1975.004. Boyte, Harry C. "The Politics of Community: The New Populism." *The Nation*, Vol. 240 (January 12, 1985), p. 12.

Boyte is describing a renewed sense of community activism in America, and recalling historical precedents, among them: "Thomas Jefferson thought that the Iroquois' primary reliance on the moral force of community opinion rather than laws to control social problems furnished the model of democratic self-government."

1975.005. Burton, Bruce. "The American Indian's Contribution to Government." *Anthropological Journal of Canada* 18:1(1980), pp. 26-28.

This article was reprinted in *Masinaigan: A Chronicle of The Lake Superior Ojibway*, July, 1987.

1975.006. Burton, Bruce. "A Film on the Founding of the Five Nations Confederacy." *International Journal of Instructional Media* 7:2(1979-1980), pp. 109-113.

This article advances the idea of such a film, given the importance of the Confederacy's influence on American democracy.

1975.007. Burton, Bruce A. *Hail! Nene Karenna, The Hymn: A Novel on the Founding of the Five Nations, 1550-1590.* Rochester, N.Y.: Security Dupont Press, 1981.

This book is the first historical novel detailing the founding of the Iroquois Confederacy, and its importance in shaping early notions of democracy.

1975.008. Burton, Bruce A. "Natural Righteousness: Iroquois Women and the United States Constitution." *Turtle Quarterly,* n.d., pp. 27-29.

See also: Burton, Bruce. "Iroquois Confederate Law and the Origins of the U.S. Constitution." *Northeast Indian Quarterly* 3:3(Fall, 1986), pp. 4-9.

1975.009. Chamberlin, J. E. *The Harrowing of Eden: White Attitudes Toward Native Americans.* A Continuum Book. New York: Seabury Press, 1975.

On page 136, Chamberlin observes that "...[I]t is generally held that the model of the great Iroquois (Six Nations) Confederacy was a significant influence on both the Albany Plan [of 1754] and the later Articles of Confederation." In a footnote (pp. 227-28), Chamberlin also notes the Iroquois influence on Marx and Engels through Lewis Henry Morgan.

1975.010. Grinde, Donald A., Jr. *The Iroquois and the Founding of the American Nation.* San Francisco: Indian Historian Press, 1977.

This was the first book-length treatment of the "influence" issue, combined with a diplomatic history of the Iroquois Confederacy in the American Revolution.

1975.011. Hamilton, Charles, ed. *The Cry of the Thunderbird: The American Indian's Own Story.* Norman: University of Oklahoma Press, 1977.

Introductory material to Chief Elias Johnson (Tuscarora), "Origin of the Five Nations," (p. 118) briefly describes how and why the Iroquois League was organized, observing: "So effective was this wilderness democracy that Benjamin Franklin recommended that the United States model its government after the League of the Iroquois."

1975.012. Johansen, Bruce and Roberto Maestas. *Wasi'chu: the Continuing Indian Wars.* New York: Monthly Review Press, 1979.

Pages 34-37 of this book contain a short description of the Great Law of Peace, and note Benjamin Franklin's reliance on it in the Albany Plan of Union, as well as Frederick Engels' description of Iroquois society and governance in *The Origin of the Family, Private Property, and the State.*

1975.013. Johansen. *Forgotten Founders: Benjamin Franklin, the Iroquois and the Rationale for the American Revolution.* Ipswich, Mass.: Gambit, 1982.

[Files contain reviews of *Forgotten Founders* from *Choice* (March, 1983), University of Nebraska at Omaha *Gateway* (January 21, 1983 and June 24, 1983), University of Washington *Daily* (July 21, 1982), *The Atlantic* (February, 1983), The Los Angeles *Times* (December 21, 1982), University of Washington *Alumnus* (Winter, 1982), *New Age* (November, 1982), *Publishers Weekly* (February 5, 1982), *Booklist* (May 15, 1982), The Boston *Globe* (November 25, 1982), The St. Louis *Post-Dispatch* (December 5, 1982), *In These Times* (May 4, 1983), The Seattle *Times* (May 30, 1982), The Milwaukee *Sentinel* (March 4, 1983), The Omaha *World-Herald* (August 14, 1983) and *The Journal of Interdisciplinary History,* n.d.]

1975.014. Johansen. "The Forgotten Founders..." *Four Winds: the International Forum of Native American Art, Literature and History* [Austin, Texas], Spring, 1982, pp. 8-14.

Excerpt from *Forgotten Founders*

1975.015. Johansen. "Mohawks, Axes & Taxes: Images of the American Revolution." *History Today* [London, England]. April, 1985, pp. 10-18.

Excerpt from work in *Exemplar of Liberty* [1991], chapter of the same name.

1975.016. Lowes, Warren. *Indian Giver: A Legacy of North American Native Peoples.* Penticton, B.C.: Theytus Books, 1986.

This book includes a chapter titled "The Influence of Folk Democracy," outlining Iroquois contributions to the development of democracy. Lowes cites Brandon [1961] and Grinde, *The Iroquois and the Founding of the American Nation* [1977]. This book has been associated with Jack Weatherford's *Indian Givers* [1988] as an object of plagiarism by Ward Churchill, *Indians Are Us? Culture and Genocide in Native North America* [1994]. Lowes cites Grinde [1977].

1975.017. Matthiessen, Peter. *Indian Country.* New York: Viking, 1979.

On page 6, Matthiessen contrasts Francis Parkman's description of the Iroquois' "homicidal fury" ("man, wolf and devil all in one") with the Iroquois' "parliamentary system, so admired by Benjamin Franklin and the Founding Fathers, [which] was incorporated into his [Parkman's] country's constitution."

1975.018. Steiner, Stan. *The Vanishing White Man.* New York: Harper & Row, 1976.

On pages 149-151, Steiner briefly recounts Cannassatego's advice that the colonists unite on an Iroquois model (1744), and Benjamin Franklin's use of Iroquois precedents in his Albany Plan of Union (1754). "The most obvious origin of the 'American Way' has been largely ignored -- the native land and the native people themselves." (p. 149). Steiner also mentions the use of a Mohawk disguise at the Boston Tea Party, and George Washington's adaptation of Native American modes of warfare.

1975.019. Wallace, Amy. *The Prodigy.* New York: E.P. Dutton, 1986.

This is a biography of William James Sidis [See Johansen, 1989]. On page 202, Wallace notes that none of the present-day scholars who have explored Native Americans' democratic traditions have heard of Sidis' earlier, unpublished work. "An excellent work, complete with footnotes [that is not true] and an extensive bibliography, is Bruce E.

Johansen's *Forgotten Founders*, published in 1982 by Gambit publishers." Ironically, Sidis' unpublished manuscript was found in Ipswich, Mass., home of Gambit, although Johansen nor Lovell Thompson, owner of Gambit, knew of it when *Forgotten Founders* was published there.

Newspaper and Trade Magazine articles

1975.020. _____.   "Smithsonian Official Talks of Indians' Historic Role."   [United Press International] October 9, 1986.

Rayna Green, director of the American Indian Program at the Smithsonian, is speaking in Eugene, Oregon. The so-called 'Founding Fathers' were backed up by others, 'forgotten founders,'" she said. She mentions the role of Benjamin Franklin.

1975.021. Bickford, Walter. "Significance of the Oneida Indian Nation Land Claim Suit." [letter to the editor] Boston *Globe*, April 15, 1985.

Bickford, commissioner of the Massachusetts Department of Fisheries, Wildlife, and Recreational Vehicles, is replying to Allen Van Gestel's March 18 opinion piece in the Boston *Globe* that argues against a land claim of the Oneida Nation. Bickford's letter concludes with a summary of Iroquois contributions to American thought. "It was as ambassadors in the 1740s to the Iroquois League that Franklin...learned of 'self-evident truths,' 'inalienable rights,' 'life, liberty, and the pursuit of happiness,' and that 'all men are created equal'....European thinkers appear to have received much inspiration from America's true founding fathers, or 'forgotten founders,' the Indians," Bickford writes.

1975.022. Cook, James. "The American Indian Through Five Centuries." *Forbes*, November 9, 1981, p. 118.

"The six Iroquois nations were among the most politically sophisticated peoples in the world, forming the famed Iroquois Confederation...that provided a model in its system of checks and balances for the U.S. Constitution." This early endorsement of the "influence" thesis in *Forbes* stood in sharp contrast to the magazine's treatment of the same idea a decade later [See D'Souza, 1991] after it had become a litmus-test issue for conservatives in the debate over multiculturalism and "political correctness."

1975.023. Gibson, Arrell. *The American Indian: Prehistory to the Present*, Lexington, Mass.: D. C. Heath, 1980.

Page 581: "Felix Cohen [1952], late international authority on Indian law and polity, has stated that 'American democracy, freedom and tolerance are more American than European and have deep aboriginal roots in our land.' The Indian example of self-determination and local sovereignty 'undoubtedly played a strong role in helping to give the colonists new sets of values that contributed to turning them from Europeans into freedom-loving Americans. And it is out of a rich democratic tradition that the distinctive political ideas of American life emerged...' The Native American contribution to the ideology of revolution in the United States, France, and Spain's New World colonies was profound."

1975.024. Johansen, Bruce. "The Indian's Past May be His Future." Seattle *Times*, May 9, 1976, pp. A-1, E-1.

Sidebar, headlined "Bicentennial? It Isn't Their Birthday Party," (on p. E-1) mentions Franklin's interest in Iroquois politics, and the Albany conference of 1754. Johansen first became acquainted with the idea of native influence on democracy from Sally Fixico, a Cherokee, who was then a student at Evergreen State College, Olympia, as he researched this newspaper series.

Files also contain a short item (no author listed), dated August 14, 1975, from an unidentified newspaper, headlined "Essay on Indian Culture by Nancy Duffy is Recognized." U.S. Congressman William F. Walsh is said to have read into *The Congressional Record* an essay by Nancy Duffy "of WHEN-TV," whose "delightful brief essay...acknowledges [that] Benjamin Franklin and Thomas Jefferson...recognized a form of democracy among the Iroquois, 'whose Five Nation League of Peace precipitated our own Constitution.'"

1975.025. Pierce, Cris. "Oldest Constitution in the World" [Letter to the editor] Los Angeles *Times*, December 14, 1985, part 2, p. 2.

Pierce says that his roots go back to the Oneida Nation of New York. Since childhood, he has been told that the Iroquois Confederacy "played a major role in shaping the ideas of the United States' founders."

Stage Play

1975.026. Script, "Night of the First Americans," performed March 4, 1982 at the Kennedy Center for the Performing Arts, Washington, D.C.

The script was written by Choctaw filmmaker Phil Lucas and included performances by a number of well-known Indian and non-Indian actors and artists, including Lorne Greene, Will Sampson, Jonathan Winters, Vincent Price, Paul Ortega, Ironeyes Cody, Martin Sheen, Dennis Weaver, Loretta Lynn, Dick Cavett, Hoyt Axton, Will Rogers, Jr., Kevin Locke, and Wayne Newton. The performance contained a substantial segment outlining the Iroquois role in the formulation of U.S. democracy. Lucas referenced working drafts of Johansen, *Forgotten Founders* [1982] for this material. Lucas and Johansen, both in Seattle at the time, were working together on the theme.

1900 - 1974

Books and Scholarly Journals

1900.001. Armstrong, Virginia Irving, comp. *I Have Spoken: American History Through the Voices of the Indians.* Chicago: Swallow Press, 1971.

In this compilation of excerpts from Native American speeches (on page 12) Armstrong writes: "Thomas Jefferson is said to have studied the Constitution of the Iroquois when it came time to frame the United States Constitution. Earlier, in 1754, when Benjamin Franklin was pleading the cause of political union of the American colonies at Albany, New York, Franklin referred to the Iroquois Confederation."

1900.002. Baity, Elizabeth Chesley. *Americans Before Columbus.* New York: Viking, 1951.

On pages 141 and 142, Baity briefly discusses Iroquois governance, and adds: "The Quakers, it has been said, borrowed [the] idea of complete agreement instead of majority rule (in political decision-making)...from the Iroquois.

1900.003. Boyd, Julian P. "Dr. Franklin: Friend of the Indian" in Ray Lokken, Jr., ed., *Meet Dr. Franklin.* Philadelphia: Franklin Institute, 1981.

Written in the early 1940s, Boyd's essay says that Franklin's 1754 Albany Plan "found his materials in the great confederacy of the Iroquois." (p. 239) Boyd was editor of Jefferson's papers and a prominent professor of history.

1900.004. Brandon, William. *The American Heritage Book of Indians.* New York: Dell, 1961.

This paperback includes an introduction by President John F. Kennedy: "....[T]he League of the Iroquois inspired Benjamin Franklin to copy it in planning the federation of States."

1900.005. Brandon, William. *The American Heritage Book of Indians.* New York: American Heritage/Simon & Schuster, 1961.

This is the coffee-table version of the previously cited paperback, with copious artwork, in a large format. It includes the John F. Kennedy assertion that Franklin used the Iroquois League as a model of American confederation (p. 7), and observations by Brandon on the appeal of liberty in the European and colonial image of American Indians. He describes the Iroquois League and its formation (pp. 175-176), and notes its use by Frederich Engels in *The Origin of Family, Private Property, and the State* (1884). Brandon also notes Native American notions of liberty in the Tammany Society and the philosophy of Rousseau.

1900.006. Cohen, Felix. "Americanizing the White Man." *The American Scholar* 21:2(1952), pp. 177-191.

Cohen, a leading scholar of Indian law of his day (and author of the *Handbook of Indian Law*), develops an evocative case for Native

American influence on American notions of liberty and federalism. This essay had the effect of spurring several later explorations of the "influence" idea.

1900.007. Grant, Bruce. *American Indians Yesterday and Today*. New York: E. P. Dutton, 1958. [Republished in 1989 by Wings Press (Random House) as *Concise Encyclopedia of the American Indian*.]

Page 169, under "Iroquois," after a brief discussion of the Iroquois League's founding:" "The 'constitution' of the Iroquois was not written, but it was greatly admired by the colonists. Many claim that this confederacy served as a pattern for the Constitution in providing the sovereign rights of states."

1900.008. Hamilton, Charles. *Cry of the Thunderbird: The American Indian's Own Story*. Norman: University of Oklahoma Press, 1972.

This is a reprint of the 1950 title, below.

1900.009. Hislop, Codman. *Rivers of America: The Mohawk*. New York: Rinehart & Co., 1948.

Page 47: "Their [the Iroquois'] Great Binding Law was said to have inspired Benjamin Franklin's plan for a union of the colonies. Through him and those other political philosophers who knew the Iroquois well it may even have helped shape the Constitution of the United States, in the morning of a new American confederacy."

1900.010. Josephy, Alvin. *The Patriot Chiefs*. New York: Viking, 1958.

In his chapter "The Real Hiawatha," Josephy discusses the Iroquois Great Law of Peace: "So unique a native organization, resting on high-minded principles of republicanism and democracy, eventually quickened the interest of many colonial leaders, including Benjamin Franklin, but the gap between the two races was too wide and dangerous in the eighteenth century to permit the study of the Iroquois system or its origins." (p. 9)

Josephy returns to the theme at the end of the chapter (pp. 28-29), writing that "Throughout the eighteenth century, the republican and democratic principles that lay at the heart of the Five Nations' system of self-government had been included among the studies of the philosophers of Europe and America who were seeking a more just and humane way for men to be governed." (p. 28) The Iroquois advised the colonists to adopt a confederacy based on their model, he says, mentioning Franklin's 1754 Albany Plan, as well as Franklin's 1751 letter to his printing partner James Parker. While Josephy maintains that "it would be impossible to trace more than an indirect influence of the Iroquois League....on the United States government as it was constituted in 1789," certain practices, such as congressional conference committees, echo the debating procedures of the Iroquois Grand Council.

1900.011. Josephy, Alvin. *The Indian Heritage of America.* New York: Bantam, 1969.

This is the paperback version of a 1968 title from Alfred A. Knopf, a general survey of Native cultures and histories. On page 33, Josephy cites Franklin's 1751 advice on emulating the Iroquois confederation. He concludes that Iroquois political structure influenced that of the United States from the Albany Congress of 1754 through the Constitutional Convention. Josephy points to the operations of congressional conference committees as an example.

1900.012. Kownslar, Allan O. *Discovering American History.* New York: Holt, Rinehart, and Winston, 1974.

This high-school history textbook pairs Benjamin Franklin's "unite or die" cartoon with an illustration of an Iroquois wampum belt, and comments: "Franklin's Albany Plan might have been inspired by the Iroquois League."

1900.013. Moquin, Wayne, ed. *Great Documents in American Indian History.* New York: Praeger, 1973.

"An Appeal for Justice" (1948), by Indians of the St. Regis Reservation, Hogansburg, New York (pp. 328-329), observes that, among many contributions of Native Americans to Euro-american culture, "[We] showed them the workings, the operation of a great democracy, the Iroquois Confederacy, a system unknown in Europe or Asia." The statement argues that many Indians fought for democracy in World

War II, and argues against termination of treaties. This statement was first published in *The American Indian* 4:3(1948).

1900.014. Morgan, Lewis Henry. *League of the Ho-de-no-sau-nee, or Iroquois* [1851]. New York: Burt Franklin, 1901.

In this edition of Morgan's classic work, editor Herbert M. Lloyd adds his annotations to two volumes. In Appendix B, page 148, Vol. 2, he writes: "In their ancient League the Iroquois presented to us the type of a Federal Republic under whose roof and around whose council-fires all peoples might dwell in peace and freedom....Our nation gathers its people from many peoples of the old world, its language and its free institutions it inherits from England, its civilization and art from Greece and Rome, its religion from Judea -- and even these red men of the forest have wrought some of the chief stones in our national temple."

1900.015. Porter, C. Fayne. *Our Indian Heritage: Profiles of Twelve Great Leaders.* New York: Chilton Books, 1964.

In its table of contents (p. ix) this book introduces Hiawatha, who "brought the Iroquois together into an early self-governing league that may have influenced the colonial Continental Congress." The chapter on Hiawatha (pp. 7-21) is titled "Father of Our Constitution?" The chapter begins with a discussion of the Founders, and asks, "What was the genesis of this revolutionary idea?" Porter surveys European antecedents (the Greeks, English, et al.) and then presents the founding story of the Iroquois Confederacy with the preface: "Relatively few serious researchers have gone into another fascinating possibility -- that these men were equally influenced by an Indian political organization...which flowered a short distance from the revolutionists...." (p. 8)   On pages 19 and 20, Porter mentions Cannassatego's advice on union during 1744 (without naming him), Franklin's letter to James Parker (1751) and Franklin's designs for the Albany Plan of Union (1754). The chapter concludes: "Perhaps it is more than coincidence that the free government of the United States was born and was nourished alongside the Federation of the Iroquois." (p. 21)

1900.016. Tebbel, John and Keith Jennison. *The American Indian Wars.* New York: Bonanza Books, 1960.

At the end of its Epilogue (pp. 300-301), this book quotes from a statement by "a young Indian private first class in the American Army, printed in the New York *Herald-Tribune* of March 14, 1960:" "The Iroquois has [*sic*] contributed much to early America. Were it not for us, the United States might not be a democracy, for democracy was unknown in the European countries from which you came, but democracy was in full flourish here on this continent."

1900.017. Tehanetorens [Ray Fadden]. *History of the Oneida Nation. Hogansburg, N.Y.:* Akwesasne Mohawk Counselor Organization, n.d.

Tehanetorens [Ray Fadden] is a teacher of many younger Mohawks, and founder of the Six Nations Indian Museum at Onchiota, N.Y. In his 80s during the 1990s, he watched ideas of Iroquois democracy spread around the world in ways that he had foreseen a half century earlier. In this short book, Tehanetorens makes a case for Iroquois influence on the development of democracy that consulted sources used to build the case in scholarly circles three decades later, such as Cadwallader Colden and Felix Cohen. He quotes from Cohen's 1952 piece in *The American Scholar:* "Politically, there was nothing in the kingdoms and empires of Europe in the 15th and 16th centuries to equal the democratic constitution of the Iroquois." Fadden, a life-long educator, inspired many younger people throughout his life.

1900.018. Underhill, Ruth. *Red Man's America: A History of Indians in the United States,* Chicago: University of Chicago Press, 1953.

This general history of Native Americans in the United States, which was reprinted in 1971, includes a description of the Iroquois Confederacy, which notes that "The Iroquois government was the most orderly north of Mexico, and some have even thought it gave suggestions to the American Constitution. (Lee, Franklin, and Jefferson were quite familiar with the League)."

1900.019. Vogel, Virgil J. *This Country Was Ours: A Documentary History of the American Indian.* New York: Harper & Row, 1974.

"Montaigne, Rousseau, and Jefferson paid tribute to the Indian capacity to organize human affairs in a libertarian manner. The Iroquois developed a system of confederated government which, according to Benjamin Franklin, served as an example for his Albany Plan of Union, and eventually for the Articles of Confederation. Felix Cohen has lashed the assumption that our democracy was born in Greece." The book (on page 298, "The Indian in Perspective,") then quotes Cohen, who wrote the landmark text on American Indian law, in his 1952 *American Scholar* article "Americanizing the White Man," [21:2(Spring, 1952), pp. 179-180]: "...it is out of a rich Indian democratic tradition that the distinctive political ideals of American life emerged. Universal suffrage for women as well as for men, the pattern of states within a state that we call federalism, the habit of treating chiefs as servants of the people instead of their masters, the insistence that the community must respect the diversity of men and the diversity of their dreams -- all these things were part of the American way of life before Columbus landed." The disguise of patriots as Mohawks at the Boston tea party is noted, as well as a verse from a poem by Robert P. Tristram Coffin:

> *We bent down to the bob-cat's crouch,*
> *Took color from the butternut tree,*
> *At Saratoga, Lexington,*
> *We fought like Indians and went free.*

1900.020. Wallace, Paul A. W. *The White Roots of Peace.* Philadelphia: University of Pennsylvania Press, 1946.

At the beginning of his introduction [page 3] Wallace writes that the "United Nations of the Iroquois...provided a model for, and an incentive to, the transformation of the thirteen colonies into the United States of America." He quotes Franklin's 1751 letter to his printing partner: "It would be a strange thing if Six Nations..." Wallace also draws a parallel between the Great Law and the United Nations Charter. This book was reprinted in 1980 by the Center for Adirondack Studies, and in 1994 by Clear Light Publishers, Santa Fe, NM.

1900.021. Wilson, Edmund. *Apologies to the Iroquois.* New York: Farrar, Straus and Cudahy, 1960.

Wilson's interest in the Iroquois was first stirred in the 1950s by a Mohawk land-rights activist named Standing Arrow, who "told me...that Benjamin Franklin had been influenced by the example of the Iroquois Confederacy in his project for uniting the American colonies. It has always, I found, been the boast of the Iroquois that our written

Constitution, with its federal authority balanced against states' rights, was derived from their unwritten one." (p. 47)

1900.022. Wissler, Clark. *Indians of the United States: Four Centuries of Their History and Culture.* Garden City, N.Y.: Doubleday, 1940.

Following a brief discussion of the Iroquois League's formation and operation on page 112, Wissler, who in 1940 was curator of anthropology at the American Museum of Natural History, writes: "There is some historical evidence that knowledge of the league influenced the colonists in their first efforts to form a confederacy and later write a constitution."

1900.023. Zolla, Elemire. *The Writer and the Shaman: A Morphology of the American Indian.* New York: Harcourt Brace Jovanovich, 1973.

On page 225, Zolla describes Edmund Wilson's introduction to the Iroquois, as he researched *Apologies to the Iroquois*: "He discovered that the Constitution of the United States was influenced by the unwritten constitution of the Iroquois Confederation, that Benjamin Franklin had been inspired by it to unify the American colonies."

Specialty Journals, Newspapers, and Newsletters

1900.024. Akweks, Aren [Ray Fadden]. "The Formation of the Ho-de-no-saune or League of the Five Nations. St. Regis, N.Y.: Akwesasne Mohawk Counselor Organization, 1948.

This brief booklet outlines Haudenosaunee political organization and history, with the this summary statement: "Their [the Iroquois'] handiwork was found to be good; so good that those who know of it cannot help but marvel; so good that its greatest features are found in the government of today's United States. Indians of today, we deserve to feel good about the great men of our history."

1900.025. Eastman, Charles. *American Indian Magazine,* 7:3(1919), pp. 145-152.

Speaking to an audience of Native American leaders, Eastman said, in part: "We Indians laid the foundation of freedom and equality long before any Europeans came and took it up, but they do not give us credit....We were [of] that character, that original American character....We must keep our heads and our hearts together, [and] keep our old characteristics that we have contributed to this country -- those contributions which have been put into the Constitution of the United States itself."

1900.026. Fenton, William N. "The Science of Anthropology and the Iroquois Indians." *Bulletin of the New York State Archaeology Society No. 6* (March, 1956), pp. 10-14.

In this paper, which was read to the WGY Science Forum, March 2, 1955, Fenton writes that "The Six Nations of the Iroquois were very much in the minds of colonial politicians, several of whom had their first lessons in diplomacy at the fire of Indian councils. The old men of the Longhouse, as they styled their confederacy, on several occasions suggested their league as a model for the thirteen colonies. And Franklin, in advancing his Plan of Union, argued: "It would be a strange thing if Six Nations...." Part of the text of Franklin's 1751 letter to his printing partner James Parker follows.

1900.027. McLellan, Howard. "Indian Magna Carta Writ in Wampum Belts." New York *Times*, June 7, 1925, n.p.

This piece, reprinted in *Akwesasne Notes* [New Series 1:3 & 4 (Fall, 1995), pp. 64-65], describes how Iroquois are using the contents of ancient wampum belts to deny that they should become United States citizens. The author calls the Iroquois League "a crude forerunner of the present League of Nations at Geneva."

1900.028. Newell, William B, ed. *The Six Nations.* 2:2(April, 1928), p. 7.

In the newsletter of The Society for the Propagation of Indian Welfare, Newell lists items that "History Books do Not Tell," among them "THAT the Iroquois Indians had one of the most remarkable political organizations ever formed and upon which the United States government is based." Files contain an undated article by Newell titled "Contributions of the American Indian to Modern Civilization."

Subject Index

Author Index

About the Compiler

BRUCE E. JOHANSEN is Professor of Communication and Native American Studies at the University of Nebraska in Omaha. He has been a participant in the debate over Native American precedents for democracy for twenty years, completing his Ph.D. dissertation on the topic in 1979. He is the author of *Forgotten Founders: Benjamin Franklin, the Iroquois, and the Rationale for the American Revolution* (1982), coauthor of *Exemplar of Liberty: Native America and the Evolution of Democracy* (1991), and author of *Debating Democracy: The Iroquois Legacy of Freedom* (forthcoming, 1996).